Knowledge
Matters

A reference guide to the theory requirements
of LAMDA Graded Examinations
in Speaking Verse and Prose
from 1 September 2009

KNOWLEDGE MATTERS
previously published as The Discussion: 1996, 2000, 2004
first published in 2009 by the
London Academy of Music and Dramatic Art
155 Talgarth Road, London W14 9DA
Tel: 0844 847 0520 / Fax: 0844 847 0521
e-mail: publications@lamda.org.uk
www.lamda.org.uk

A catalogue record for this book is available from the British Library.

EDITOR: Greg Hamerton
SUB-EDITOR: Ann Newson
CONTRIBUTORS: Mia Ball, Valerie King, Paul Ranger, Godfrey Salter, Pauline Stephens, Michael Stone, Sherna Treherne, Sean McKenna, The Voice Care Network UK, Catherine Weate and Lucy Atkinson (illustrations).

COVER IMAGE: The handwriting of John Keats, from an original manuscript.

ISBN: 978-0-95576873-6

CONTENTS

INTRODUCTION

We have called this book *Knowledge Matters* because knowledge of interpretative skills, technical skills and literature is the foundation for performance. This is a reference book for teachers and students of speech and drama and an essential guide for learners studying for the LAMDA *Graded Examinations in Communication: Speaking Verse and Prose (from 1 September 2009)*. It provides the necessary information on the set theory for the various grades.

Graded Examinations in Communication: Speaking Verse and Prose

The examinations have been designed to develop the skills necessary for effective oral communication of the written word. *Knowledge Matters* should be read in conjunction with the syllabus for *Graded Examinations in Speech: Speaking Verse and Prose*, which is available to download from LAMDA's website or to purchase in printed form.

The examinations are divided into four distinct levels, in line with the Qualifications and Credit Framework.

National Qualifications	LAMDA Grades
Entry Level	Entry
Level 1	Grade 1
	Grade 2
	Grade 3
Level 2	Grade 4
	Grade 5
Level 3	Grade 6 – Bronze Medal
	Grade 7 – Silver Medal
	Grade 8 – Gold Medal

The set theory is listed in the Knowledge section of each grade within the syllabus.

The Knowledge section

The set knowledge has been designed to introduce learners to the technical aspects of performing verse and prose. The learner's knowledge is tested in discussion with the examiner after the learner has performed their chosen selections. The examiner will aim to set the learner at ease. Questioning is more formal in the higher grades as the set knowledge requirements increase in technical difficulty.

The examiner will initiate the discussion and the learner will be encouraged to respond. This should evolve into a two-way exchange between the examiner and the learner, during which the learner will be given every opportunity to share their knowledge.

There is a time limit for the knowledge section. However, the learner must be prepared to discuss all aspects of the requirements for the grade being assessed, including that set for previous grades.

The examiner will base their questions on the set knowledge requirements printed in the syllabus for *Graded Examinations in Communication: Speaking Verse and Prose (from 1 September 2009)*. This information should be made available to the learner by the teacher so that the learner is fully prepared and is able to discuss the theory with confidence.

Practical application

This book has been designed to help the learner to understand and use background knowledge and techniques required to give a creative, enhanced performance.

Practical application of the knowledge learnt and understood will lead to a greater enjoyment of verse and prose in performance. It is therefore important that the learner relates the set knowledge to their performance as much as possible in their responses. This is particularly relevant at Grade Four (figures of speech), Grade Five (phrasing and pausing), Grade Seven (emphasis and modulation), and Grade Eight (versification) where the learner will be asked to illustrate the information with examples from their chosen selections whenever possible.

The content of this book will enable the student of speech and drama to appreciate the need for unity between knowledge and creativity.

ENTRY

Questions will be based on the following:

- *The meaning and general content of the chosen selections*
- *The meaning of individual words in both selections.*

The meaning of the poems

When you have chosen your poems, try to explore their meaning. It is important to understand them as a whole.
For example:

- Do they paint a picture?
- Do they tell a story?
- What are the poems trying to say?

The meaning of the words

To understand the whole of the poem you must know the meanings of all the words. If you are uncertain of any words try not to guess the meaning but look them up in a dictionary. Some words have more than one meaning and you can only tell which one you want from the way the word is used within the surrounding text.

GRADE ONE

Questions will be based on the following:

- *The mood, content and contrast between the selections*
- *The meaning of the chosen selections*
- *The meaning of individual words in both selections.*

The learner must be prepared to discuss with the examiner any aspect of theory specified for previous grades.

Mood, content, contrast

For your examination, select two pieces of verse that differ in either theme or mood so that you are able to show some contrast when you perform them. Remember, it is possible to have two very different approaches to the same subject.

To prepare, you should look at the way the pieces are written. For example:

- Are they shaped differently on the page?
- Do they have a strong rhythm?
- Do they both use rhyme?
- What is the mood of each poem?
- Is the mood different in the two poems?

One may be humorous, the other more serious; one could be scary and the other bright and cheerful. You may also enjoy and comment on the sounds of the words in a poem.

GRADE TWO

Questions will be based on the following:

- *An outline of the story of the book from which the prose selection has been taken.*

The learner must be prepared to discuss with the examiner any aspect of theory specified for previous grades.

An outline of the story

When you have read your book, try to answer these questions:

- What happens in the story?
- Where and when is the story set?
- Do you have a favourite part of the story?
- How does the extract you are performing fit into the story as a whole?

When discussing your book with the examiner, remember to answer the questions as fully as possible whilst being concise.

GRADE THREE

Questions will be based on the following:

- *Two characters in the story from which the prose selection has been taken*
- *The fundamental differences between verse and prose.*

The learner must be prepared to discuss with the examiner any aspect of theory specified for previous grades.

Choice of characters

When you have read your book and chosen two characters, think about the following questions:

- Why have you chosen them?
- Are these main characters in the story?
- What do you think these characters look like?
- What do they say about themselves?
- What happens to them and why?
- Do they know each other?

The fundamental differences between verse and prose

Prose is the usual form of written and spoken language. In English, words flow continuously across the page and are broken into sentences and paragraphs. Prose writing usually follows a logical sequence and a grammatical order.

Verse is immediately recognisable on the page because the words are arranged into patterns. Verse may be broken up into stanzas but this is not essential. Verse often has little grammatical order. Insignificant but grammatically necessary words may be omitted and the accepted word order changed. In some modern verse there is little or no punctuation and even a lack of capital letters. Verse may also make more use of figures of speech, such as similes and metaphors, than prose. Verse often rhymes at line endings.

Examples of different verse patterns:
Testing by Bob Sparrow
Snow by Walter de la Mare.

Prose and **verse** both possess rhythm but verse rhythm is more distinct. Rhythm is the beat or pulse you can hear when you say the words. Sometimes the rhythm is arranged in a regular pattern of stressed and unstressed syllables, which is known as **metre**. Verse rhythm can be very strong and easy to feel or quite gentle and subtle.

Verse examples can be found in *The LAMDA Verse and Prose Anthology (Volume 17).*

Some examples of verse with a strong metrical rhythm are:
The Witch by Mary Elizabeth Coleridge
The Dentist and the Crocodile by Roald Dahl.

GRADE FOUR

Questions will be based on the following:

- *The relationship between two characters of the learner's own choice in the story from which the prose selection has been taken*
- *Figures of speech (alliteration, assonance, onomatopoeia, antithesis, pun, simile, metaphor, personification).*

Definitions must be illustrated with examples from the chosen selections where possible. The learner must be prepared to discuss with the examiner any aspect of theory specified for previous grades.

The relationship between two characters

When you have read your book and chosen two characters, try to think about the following questions:

- What do the characters say about each other?
- What do other people say about them?
- How do the characters relate to each other?
- How does their relationship develop or change and why?

Figures of speech

A figure of speech is a non-literal expression or one which uses a particular pattern of words for emphasis. Such features are found more commonly in verse than prose, though some are used quite regularly in everyday speech without being recognised for what they are.

(a) Alliteration. Alliteration is the repetition of an initial consonant. This can produce a striking effect when the poem is spoken aloud. One example of the repetition of the crisp 'k' sound is found in the opening line of T.S. Eliot's *The Journey of the Magi.*

A cold coming we had of it...

Leonard Clark uses the liquid 'l' sound for a smoother effect in *Singing in the Streets.*

Firelight, lamplight, the little lame cat...

(b) Assonance. Assonance, less commonly used than alliteration, is the repetition of a vowel sound, and again it is particularly noticeable when the lines are spoken. The short 'i' is used in *Lizard* by Moira Andrew, which accentuates the quick movement of the lizard.

...a flicker of light,
a gleam of gold
    glittering
just out of sight.

The opening lines of Coleridge's *Kubla Khan* provide a good example of alliteration and assonance combined.

In Xanadu did Kubla Khan
A stately pleasure dome decree:
Where Alph, the sacred river, ran
Through caverns measureless to man
Down to a sunless sea.

(c) Onomatopoeia. Onomatopoeia is another device which makes particular use of sounds, as it refers to those words that make a sound similar to their meaning when spoken aloud. Among the simplest are 'pop' and 'hiss'. There are relatively few words which really fulfil this criterion but in poetry there is often an onomatopoeic quality to phrases which enhance the meaning when spoken. One example is from Wilfred Owen's

Anthem for Doomed Youth.

> The stuttering rifles' rapid rattle...

Brian Lee's *Night Music* also concentrates on sound.

> A door clicks; and swishes open, on its own...
> Milk bottles tinkle on a step. A window shrieks
> Upwards; the bath-tap whispers as it leaks...

(d) Antithesis. Antithesis occurs when a word, phrase or idea is set in opposition to another, resulting in a strong contrast or ambiguity which can often surprise or shock. In its simplest form it is the placing of opposites beside one another, as in Henrietta Stickland's *Dinosaur Roar.*

> Dinosaur roar, dinosaur squeak,
> Dinosaur fierce, dinosaur meek...

It is quite a dramatic device and often used by Shakespeare. A more striking and developed example of antithesis can be seen in one of Romeo's speeches from the first scene of *Romeo and Juliet.*

> Here's much to do with hate, but more with love.
> Why then, O brawling love! O loving hate
> O anything, of nothing first create!
> O heavy lightness! Serious vanity!

(e) Pun. A pun plays with the meanings of words. It uses a word which has two different meanings both of which are relevant in the context. This ambiguity is often humorous, as in Richard Edwards' poem *Waterway Robbery*, which is about a carp who has to pay money to the more dominant pike.

> "Thank goodness," the carp thought,
> "That rivers have banks!"

(f) Simile. A simile is one of the most commonly used figures of speech, likening one thing to another thing. One simple and well-known example is the opening line of Robert Burns' poem:

My love is like a red, red rose.

A more unusual simile is found in Berlie Doherty's *Quieter than Snow*, where she writes:

Silence hung in the yard like sheets.

You can always recognise a simile by the use of the words 'like' or 'as'.

(g) Metaphor. A metaphor is more powerful than a simile as it turns one thing into something else. A clear example comes in Shakespeare's *Othello*, when Iago speaks:

O, beware, my lord, of jealousy;
It is the green-eyed monster, which doth mock
The meat it feeds on.

Some metaphors are extended through a whole piece of writing. In Andrew Young's *Hard Frost*, the frost is seen as an army and the image is sustained through the whole poem.

> Look for examples of all these features in your chosen verse. Be prepared to talk through these examples with the examiner.

PERSONIFICATION

GRADE FIVE

Questions will be based on the following:

- *The main plot of the book from which the prose selection has been taken, its development and outcome*
- *Phrasing (sense-groups, breath groups, parenthesis)*
- *Pausing (sense pause, emphatic pause, rhythmical or metrical pause, suspensory pause, caesural pause, emotional pause). Definitions must be illustrated with examples from the chosen selections where possible.*

The learner must be prepared to discuss with the examiner any aspect of theory specified for previous grades.

The plot of the book

The plot is a narrative of events with emphasis on cause and effect: what happened, and why? It is the way that a story is arranged. For example, important information may be withheld from the reader or the story might not be told in chronological order.

In the classical novel, *Jane Eyre* by Charlotte Bronte, the existence of Mrs Rochester is crucial to the story, although in terms of the plot it is not divulged until half way through the book.

E M Forster defined the difference between a story and a plot. 'A story is a narrative of events in chronological order. A plot is a narrative of events with the emphasis on causality.'

Phrasing

Grammatically, a **phrase** is a group of words which make sense but not complete sense on their own. For example:

> The captain *of the ship* has gone on board.
> Jack was found *after a long search.*

In speech, a **phrase** consists of a group of words linked together by sense. Phrases are sometimes called 'sense-groups'.

(a) Sense-groups. Each sense-group introduces a fresh idea. The sense-group may be one word or a number of words. To break a sense-group is to destroy the sense.

In the beginning of *Water Picture* by May Swenson, we read:

In the pond in the park	[sense-group]
all things are doubled:	[sense-group]
Long buildings hang and	
wriggle gently.	[sense-group]

(b) Breath-groups. Breath-groups and sense-groups frequently coincide, but this is not a rule. The breath-group represents the number of sense-groups that can easily be said on one breath. The ability to adjust breathing to meet the demands of the breath-group depends on an understanding of phrasing and breath control. Breath pauses may be longer than sense pauses and should occur where a longer pause is indicated by the text (often by punctuation, for example a comma or a full stop).

Notice how the breath-groups are slightly altered:

In the pond in the park	
all things are doubled:	[breath-group]
Long buildings hang and	
wriggle gently.	[breath-group]

(c) Parenthesis. Parenthesis occurs when a word, phrase or sentence is inserted as an explanation, afterthought or an aside into a passage which is grammatically complete without it. It is usually marked by brackets, dashes, or commas. Parenthesis can be made clear in performance with a pause before and after the group of words, or with a change in pitch, pace or volume.

In *The No. 1 Ladies' Detective Agency* by Alexander McCall Smith, there is a clear example of parenthesis – the phrase between the two commas.

> Then, moving as slowly as she could, she eased herself into the driving seat and reached forward to turn the key.

Pausing

In speech, a **pause** is when sound stops. There are many different types of pauses which help the speaker or reader to bring meaning and mood to life.

(a) The Sense Pause. The sense pause is used in connected speech to mark the sense by indicating the end or beginning of a sense-group. It is sometimes referred to as oral punctuation, but this can be misleading as it would seem to imply that it is used in the same places as written punctuation, which is not always the case.

(b) The Emphatic Pause. A pause for emphasis may be made before a word or phrase, after the word or phrase, or, for extra strong emphasis, both before and after the word or phrase. The word or phrase is therefore isolated and achieves prominence. Carefully timed, an emphatic pause will build suspense and climax. Holding an emphatic pause for too long will break the sense and alienate an audience.

Observe how effective an empathic pause is when used before

the final word of the extract from *The Ratcatcher* by Roald Dahl. The Ratcatcher holds up a rat and a ferret, separated by inches.

> "Now," he said. "Watch!"

(c) The Emotional Pause. In an emotional pause the voice is suspended by the strong working of the emotions. It must be used with great subtlety or it will sound over-dramatic and insincere.

In *Noughts and Crosses* by Malorie Blackman, there is an emotional pause before the single spoken word.

> And even in this light, I could tell something was wrong. My arms dropped to my sides.

> "Callum?"

(d) The Rhythmical or Metrical Pause. Rhythmical pauses are used at the ends of lines of verse and between stanzas to indicate the form and pattern of the verse. These pauses should be timed with the rhythm of the verse. A metrical pause is also used when a line of verse is shorter than the surrounding lines so that a pause is needed to balance the rhythm and timing.

Observe the rhythmical pauses in *Black Monday Lovesong*:

In love's dances, in love's dances,	[short pause]
One retreats and one advances.	[short pause]
One grows warmer and one colder,	[short pause]
One more hesitant, one bolder.	[short pause]

(e) The Caesural Pause. A caesura is a slight pause which occurs mid-line in verse, usually indicated by a break in sense and sometimes indicated by a punctuation mark. This can be seen in *Water Picture* by May Swenson in the middle of each stanza:

The arched stone bridge
is an eye, with underlid
in the water. In its lens   [caesural pause on full-stop]
dip crinkled heads with hats

(f) The Suspensory Pause. A suspensory pause is indicated by no punctuation at the end of a line of verse, also known as an enjambed line. When it occurs in verse the speaker needs to preserve the meaning without losing the rhythm or form of the verse. The last word of the first line is suspended by pitch and length, in other words, a pause on the word itself. Therefore the speaker must continue on to the next line without a breath pause.

In *Mirage* by Philip R Rush, lines 6 and 7 are enjambed and thus include a suspensory pause on the word 'sheet':

And rejoice to see the lustrous sheet
Of water on the horizon bare.

Line structures in verse which affect pausing

(a) End-stopping. In an end-stopped line the sense and rhythm fall silent, or pause, at the end of the line. This is often indicated by a punctuation mark.

(b) Enjambment. In an enjambed line the sense of a line of verse continues onto the next line (the opposite of end-stopping).

Now try to find examples of these definitions in your chosen selections.

GRADE SIX – BRONZE MEDAL

Questions will be based on the following:

- *The key themes in the book from which the prose selection has been taken*
- *Breathing, voice and basic speech production, resonance and projection.*

The learner must be prepared to discuss with the examiner any aspect of theory specified for previous grades.

Themes in the book

Themes are related to plot. A theme is a recurring idea or subject in the novel. They may be broad (business replacing culture) or specific (the effect of hunger on honesty). Themes unite the characters, events and structure. For example, the events could all involve love, marriage, greed or adventure. Exploring a theme does not necessarily mean coming to any firm conclusion about it. For example, in the novel, *Life of Pi* by Yann Martel, the writer explores various religious views without prescribing one faith for mankind or even deciding on a single faith for himself.

Breathing

'Breath is fundamental to life. It is also fundamental to producing voice. Because breathing is an involuntary activity, we seldom give it a thought unless it is difficult or painful. But if we hear that our voice is too soft, fades away or won't carry, we need to consider how we breathe.'

[More Care for Your Voice by the Voice Care Network UK]

There are numerous bones, muscles and nerves involved in the breathing process.

(a) Bones. The spine is made up of a series of vertebrae. The twelve pairs of thoracic vertebrae curve around to the front of the chest forming the rib cage. Seven pairs join with the sternum. Three pairs join with the seventh and two pairs are 'floating' (unattached). You can feel the definition of the ribs with your fingers.

(b) Muscles. *The Intercostal Muscles* are situated between the ribs (inter = between, costal = ribs). *The Diaphragm* is a dome-shaped muscle dividing the chest and the abdomen. It is attached to the lower edges of the rib cage, the point of the sternum and, at the back, the vertebrae. *The Abdominal Muscles* form part of the abdominal cavity and help to control the movement of the diaphragm.

(c) Breathing in. The intercostal muscles contract and move the ribs slightly upwards and outwards. The diaphragm, which is attached to the ribs, moves in response to this action, flattening out. This creates more space inside the chest, giving the lungs room to expand. As the lungs expand, the air pressure reduces. Air immediately flows in through the nose or mouth in order to equalise the pressure. The abdominal muscles release and the lungs fill with air.

(d) Breathing out. We then exhale. The muscles converge simultaneously to support the release of the breath. The abdominal muscles contract, the diaphragm rises and the rib cage returns to its original position through the relaxation of the intercostals. The lungs are compressed, and air flows out through the nose and mouth, powered by the abdominal muscles.

(e) Support. Your teacher may have given you a direction to 'support your voice'. This means having just the right amount of pressure from the abdominal muscles to create just the right amount of breath force for the sound you want to use. For example, if you want to project your voice across a large space or to sustain a long phrase, then you will need a more consistent pressure from the abdominal muscles.

Breathing exercises will help you with this process. These should be preceded by relaxation exercises. When you practise a breathing exercise, place your hands on your lower abdomen and centre your attention there. This will help the abdominal muscles to release on the in-breath and contract on the out-breath. Taking breath from your 'centre' (an imaginary point inside your body below your navel) will also help you to relax and release the sound more freely and easily.

(f) Clavicular breathing. To be avoided. This means moving the ribs upwards but not outwards when breathing in, holding air in the upper lungs and raising the shoulders. This sometimes happens when the body is tense, putting strain on the vocal folds. Make sure that your spine is lengthened, and your shoulders, neck and jaw are free from tension.

Voice production

'Voice begins with an impulse from the brain. It is stimulated by an intention to speak or sing. Two elements produce voice – a flow of air and vibration.

The air flows from breath. Air is taken in through the mouth or nose, passes down the trachea (or wind-pipe) and into the lungs. It is drawn there by the contraction of the dome-like diaphragm. As the diaphragm relaxes, the abdominal muscles work to return breath up the trachea.

The larynx (or voice box) is located in the upper part of the trachea. Its primary biological function is to serve as a protective valve for the air-way. When we use our voice, we close two bands of muscular tissue in the larynx – the vocal folds (or cords) – across the air flow. The out-breath causes the edges of the folds to vibrate, generating sound, in a manner similar to that of air escaping from the neck of a balloon as it deflates. The edges of the vocal cords are quite short (15 – 20 mm) and their vibration is extremely rapid. Depending on age, sex, health and the note pitched, the vocal folds may open and close between 60 and 1000 times per second.'

[More Care for Your Voice by the Voice Care Network UK]

Figure 1
The larynx (from the side)

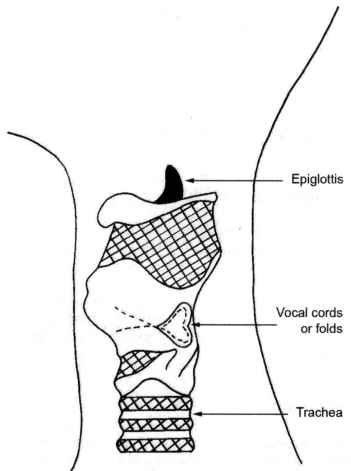

Figure 2
The larynx (from above)

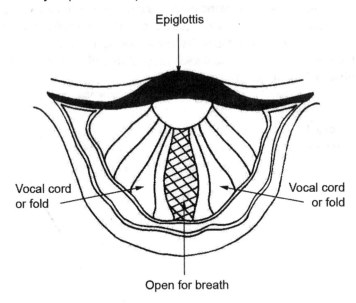

Basic speech production

Sound is turned into speech by using the organs of articulation. These are the tongue, the teeth, the teeth ridge and the hard and soft palates.

A vowel sound is an *unobstructed* sound formed by the changing shape of the mouth. A consonant sound is an *obstructed* sound formed by the use of the speech organs (organs of articulation).

Resonance

The note created in the vocal folds is then carried by the breath through various hollow spaces: the **pharynx** (or pharyngeal resonator), the **mouth** (or oral resonator) and the **nose** (or nasal resonator). The note is strengthened, amplified and given texture as it travels through these spaces.

(a) The Pharynx (pharyngeal resonator). This is the long muscular tube which extends upwards from the larynx, ending at the back part of the oral and nasal cavities. It is the first resonating space through which the note must pass on its way to the mouth and nose.

The pharynx can change its shape and size, which affects the quality of the sound produced. It increases in size during a yawn and decreases in size when the throat or neck is tense.

> Try this: Hold a yawn in your throat and count 'one, two, three' at the same time. You will hear a sound with too much pharyngeal resonance.

(b) The Mouth (oral resonator). The many parts of the mouth each play a part in producing resonance.

The lower jaw forms the floor of the oral resonator and is attached to the facial bones by hinge joints.

The tongue lies on the floor of the oral resonator, rooted in the front wall of the pharynx. It is capable of intricate and rapid movements. The movement is centred in different areas: the tip (point of the tongue), the blade (underneath the upper tooth ridge), the front (underneath the hard palate), the centre (partly underneath the hard palate and partly underneath the soft palate) and the back (underneath the soft palate).

The lips form the exit of the oral resonator at the free edges of the mouth and grip, direct and shape the breath stream.

The hard palate is an arched bone structure, separating the oral cavity from the nasal cavities, forming the roof of the mouth.

The soft palate forms the back third of the roof of the mouth, continuing from the curve of the hard palate. The back edge is free and can move up and down. Its movement controls the flow of air through the nose or mouth, like a trap door.

When breathing naturally through the nose, the soft palate is relaxed and droops down into the mouth, which leaves the passage to the nose free. When there is an impulse to speak, the soft palate contracts upwards, blocking the passage to the nose, so that the air and sound flows through the mouth.

> Try this: Say the long vowel sound 'ah' with your lower jaw dropped at its most natural point. Continue saying the sound and raise your lower jaw slowly. As the lower jaw comes up, the lips will move closer together and the tongue might move towards the hard palate. You will hear a sound without much oral resonance.

Breath carries the sound from the pharynx into the mouth. If the breath force is strong enough the sound will bounce off the hard palate and out through the lips. This is called *forward resonance*.

If the breath force is too weak to reach the hard palate, it may pitch onto the soft palate, which will make the sound difficult to project.

The mouth is capable of assuming a wide range of sizes and shapes because of the movement of the tongue, lips, jaw and soft palate. However, there needs to be space inside the mouth to create an appropriate amount of oral resonance.

> Try this: Allow your lower jaw to drop at its most natural point and use a mirror to look through to the back of the mouth. If you breathe through your nose and out through your mouth with your mouth still open then you will see the action of the soft palate.

(c) The Nose (nasal resonator).

There are two types of nasal resonance:

- When the vibrating column of air passes directly through the open soft palate to the nasal cavity. In English this only happens on three sounds - 'm', 'n' and 'ng'.
- When the vibrating column of air does not pass directly into the nasal cavity, but instead pitches onto the hard palate just behind the upper teeth, and the sound vibrations are carried through the bones of the hard palate to the nasal cavities. This type of nasal resonance can be heard in vowel sounds.

To produce the first type of nasal resonance the soft palate must be in good working order and to produce the second type of nasal resonance there must be forward resonance (the breath force is strong enough to bounce the sound off the hard palate).

If the speaker has a cold and the nasal cavities are blocked then there won't be any nasal resonance. If the soft palate doesn't close properly then too much nasal resonance will leak into the sound.

> Try this: Say 'mum', 'nose' and 'sing'. Repeat the words but this time hold your nose. You should hear 'bub', 'dose' and 'sig' because there isn't any nasal resonance.

(d) Balancing resonance. Good resonance depends upon achieving a balance of vibration from the pharynx, mouth and nose. The quality of the sound will be affected if there is too much resonance from just one of the resonators.

When you practise your exercises, make sure that your spine is lengthened, your shoulders, neck and jaw are free from tension, there is space inside your mouth and an adequate breath force to move the sound forward. It is important that you try not to think about all of this theory when you are speaking or performing. You must practice your exercises so that it comes to you naturally.

The quality of sound will also be affected if the resonators are unhealthy (e.g. if you have a cold or sore throat). Unfortunately there is little you can do to counteract the effects of illness on the quality of the sound.

Figure 3
The nose, mouth and pharynx

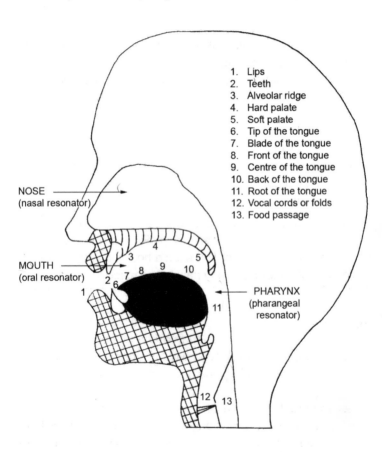

(e) Head and chest resonance. You may also feel vibrations from higher notes in your head and vibrations from lower notes in your chest when you speak, which are sometimes called head resonance and chest resonance. However, the head and chest are not official resonators as the vibrations come from sound waves produced by pharyngeal, oral and nasal resonance. For this reason, head and chest resonance are sometimes referred to as *secondary resonance*.

Projection

Projection involves:

(a) Audibility
- Strong, secure breath (breath supported by the abdominal, diaphragmatic and intercostal muscles and released freely and easily)
- Forward placement of resonance (air and sound brought forward in the mouth, using the hard palate as a sounding board).

(b) Intelligibility
- Clarity of speech (tongue and lip muscularity; precise articulation)
- Appropriate emphasis and modulation (varying use of stress, volume, pace, pitch, inflection, tone colour and pausing, according to the thought and emotion being expressed).

(c) Mental projection
- Engaging the audience by commanding their attention, which ensures that the emotion of the words is conveyed clearly.

GRADE SEVEN – SILVER MEDAL

The learner may be asked about any or all of the following:

- *The text and subtext of the book from which the prose selection has been taken and its context within it*
- *Specific verse forms (blank verse, free verse and sonnet form)*
- *Emphasis and modulation (which includes stress, volume, pace, rate, pitch, inflection, tone colour and intensity).*

Definitions must be illustrated with examples from the chosen pieces. The learner must be prepared to discuss with the examiner any aspect of theory specified for previous grades.

Text, subtext and context

Text is the main body of the writing. It is the actual words of the book.

Subtext is the *internal* world. It is the hidden meaning involving knowledge, emotion and motivation. For example, in the book *Animal Farm* by George Orwell the story is about animals acting and reacting to each other, on the surface. The underlying message (the subtext) refers to the behaviour of human beings.

Context is the *external* world. It is the choice of the setting for the novel; the social, historical and political background suited to the author's intention. It is the real world around the characters.

Specific verse forms

(a) Blank verse. Blank verse consists of a succession of unrhymed lines which have a regular rhythm. It creates a sense of simplicity and directness, perfect for character speech and dramatic performance. Shakespeare even mentions the term in *Hamlet*.

Hamlet:
> The lady shall say her mind freely, or the
> Blank verse shall halt for it.

Sometimes the occasional change to the rhythm is added, in order to create variety. Hermione's trial speech in *The Winter's Tale* is in blank verse but includes a metrical change in the fifth line, which strengthens her sense of innocence.

Hermione:
> Since what I am to say, must be but that
> Which contradicts my accusation, and
> The testimony on my part, no other
> But what comes from myself, it shall scarce boot me
> To say 'not guilty';

(b) Free verse. It is a common misconception that free verse is without form. Free verse possesses a structure but it is much more open and less bound by classical rules.

Free verse is not necessarily confined to a specific metrical law but uses a rhythm most suitable for the expression of a particular thought and emotion. For example, if the thought or emotion is profound then the rhythm will move slowly; if the thought or emotion is trivial then the rhythm will gallop along. A rhythmical unit of free verse is not a line, but a stanza, or even the whole poem itself.

Rhyme can be included in free verse but is usually a necessary part of the thought and/or emotion. Free verse came into its own in the early twentieth century with the modernist movement. T S Eliot's *Love Song of J Alfred Prufrock* is a particular example.

Let us go then, you and I,
When the evening is spread out against the sky
Like a patient etherised upon a table;

Or Walt Whitman's *Out of the Cradle Endlessly Rocking,* taken from *Leaves of Grass.*

Till of a sudden,
May-be kill'd, unknown to her mate,
One forenoon the she-bird crouch'd not on the nest,
Nor return'd that afternoon, nor the next,
Nor ever appear'd again.

And thenceforward, all summer, in the sound of the sea,
And at night, under the full of the moon, in calmer weather,
Over the hoarse surging of the sea,
Or flitting from brier to brier by day,
I saw, I heard at intervals, the remaining one, the he-bird
The solitary guest from Alabama.

(c) Sonnet form

- **The Petrarchan or Italian Sonnet.** The sonnet form is of Italian origin dating back to the Renaissance and was used by both Petrarch and Dante. The Petrarchan Sonnet consists of fourteen lines divided into an octave and a sestet. The octave is made up of two quatrains (or sets of four lines). The sestet is composed of two tercets (or sets of three lines).

  When the sonnet is written in Italian the rhyming scheme is limited. In the octave only two rhymes are the norm: *abba abba.* Three pairs of rhymes are found in the tercet: *cde cde.*

The *subject* consists of one idea which is stated boldly (often in universal terms) in the first quatrain and developed in the second. A pause then follows. In each of the two tercets the subject is again considered but particular details are shown. Finally it is brought to a definite and forceful close.

The Petrarchan Sonnet was introduced from Italy into England by Sir Thomas Wyatt and developed by Henry Howard, Earl of Surrey. Difficulties were encountered. Italian is a musical and flexible language, far more so than English, and in order to accommodate the language change extra rhymes had to be incorporated. A second change in the form was the rearrangement of the sestet in a variety of ways: sometimes the change would be in the rhyming scheme which was altered to *cd cd cd* with the sense continued in the series of three couplets (a set of two lines) instead of spread over two tercets. In England the form became more flexible than in Italy.

An example of the English development of the Petrarchan Sonnet is William Wordsworth's *Upon Westminster Bridge*.

> Earth has not anything to show more fair:
> Dull would he be of soul who could pass by
> A sight so touching in its majesty:
> This city now doth, like a garment, wear
> The beauty of the morning; silent, bare,
> Ships, towers, domes, theatres, and temples lie
> Open unto the fields, and to the sky:
> All bright and glittering in the smokeless air.
> Never did sun more beautifully steep
> In his first splendour, valley, rock, or hill:
> Ne'er saw I, never felt, a calm so deep!
> The river glideth at his own sweet will:
> Dear God! The very houses seem asleep;
> And all that mighty heart is lying still.

- **The Shakespearean Sonnet.** William Shakespeare departed from the tightly interlaced model of the Petrarchan sonnet and in its place he used a form which, although it still consists of an octave and a sestet with a pause between the two, breaks into different shapes:

  - The octave is divided into two quatrains, made distinct by the rhyme scheme which runs: *abab cdcd*
  - The sestet consists of a quatrain, *efef*, and a final couplet, *gg*

This pattern allows Shakespeare:

  - To present an argument in the octave
  - To recognise either a development or a contradiction of this in the first four lines of the sestet
  - To make a strong concluding statement in the couplet.

This is particularly evident in *Sonnet 97*.

How like a winter hath my absence been
From thee, the pleasure of the fleeting year!
What freezings have I felt, what dark days seen,
What old December's bareness everywhere!
And yet this time removed was summer's time,
The teeming autumn big with rich increase
Bearing the wanton burden of the prime,
Like widowed wombs after their lords' decease:
Yet this abundant issue seemed to me
But hope of orphans, and unfathered fruit;
For summer and his pleasures wait on thee,
And thou away, the very birds are mute;
Or if they sing, 'tis with so dull a cheer
That leaves look pale, dreading the winter's near.

Emphasis

Emphasis is when a speaker attaches extra prominence to a particular word or thought. It can be achieved through:

- Modulation (varying use of stress, volume, pace, pitch, inflection, tone colour and pausing)
- Lengthening individual sounds
- Intensity.

For example, dramatic emphasis can be achieved by increasing the intensity of the breath force, building volume and widening the pitch range.

If there is *under emphasis*, speech becomes dull, flat and monotonous. Sometimes, in certain types of humour, it can be used effectively but this should be thought of as a technique rather than the normal means of communication.

If there is *over emphasis*, speech becomes irritating and tiring to listen to.

Modulation

Modulation refers to the variations in voice and speech used by the speaker to convey meaning, mood and emotion. This includes varying the use of stress, volume, pace, pitch, inflection, tone colour and pausing.

(a) Stress. Stress is when prominence is given to a particular word or syllable, usually through a combination of extra breath force, a change in pitch and a lengthening of sound.

- **Word stress.** Every word of more than one syllable has its own stress, for example: dragon. Some words change meaning according to word stress, for example: subject (meaning a course of study) / subject (meaning to cause somebody to undergo something unpleasant). Compound words usually bear double stress, for example: home|made

- **Sentence stress.** When words are linked together, word stress changes under the influence of sentence stress. Sentence stress depends on two things:

  - The relative importance of words in the sentence, which can affect their meaning. The more important the word, the stronger its stress. For example:
    Did she give you the book? No, <u>he</u> gave me the book.
    Did you steal the book? No, he <u>gave</u> me the book.
    Is the book hers? No, he gave <u>me</u> the book.
    Did he give you the pen? No, he gave me the <u>book</u>.

  - The rhythm of the sentence can be changed by varying the stress. For example:
    In the <u>dark</u>, dark <u>wood</u> sat a <u>cruel</u> <u>hairy</u> <u>giant</u>.
    In the <u>dark</u>, dark <u>wood</u> sat a <u>cruel</u> hairy <u>giant</u>.

(b) Volume. Volume refers to the level of loudness or softness with which words are spoken. There should be constant fluctuations of volume to create a well-modulated delivery but for most work (especially verse speaking) there should be only the gentlest crescendo (becoming louder) and diminuendo (becoming softer). If too much breath force is used then shouting will occur. Shouting lacks subtlety and can create vocal problems.

(c) Pace. Pace variation is integral to the communication of meaning and mood. There should be constant fluctuations of pace to create a well-modulated delivery.

A slower pace can be achieved by lengthening vowels and continuant consonants, and lengthening the space between words. Words suggesting size, effort, astonishment and long periods of time can be taken more slowly. Meaningful and emotional passages tend to be taken at a slower pace. A phrase which contains several ideas might also be taken more slowly and deliberately than one with a simple idea.

A faster pace can be achieved by shortening vowel sounds and continuant consonants, and shortening the space between words. Quick, easy, ordinary things can be taken more rapidly. An increase in pace can also be used to build to a climax. Pace is affected by the distribution of stresses in a phrase. Lighter stressing and a more rhythmical distribution of stresses can be taken at a swifter pace.

(d) Tempo or rate. Tempo is the overall rate, or time signature, of the writing. Pace will fluctuate considerably within the limits of the tempo used by the speaker and set by the writer.

(e) Pitch. Pitch is the specific level of highness or lowness in a speech note. A higher pitch is often used for lighter and happier thoughts. A lower pitch is often used for sombre and sad thoughts.

(f) Inflection. Inflection refers to the rise and fall in pitch of the voice during speech. As the voice rises and falls it tends to form patterns or tunes. The two most commonly heard tunes are called Falling Tune and Rising Tune.

Falling Tune. This is a simple falling pattern where the stressed syllables descend from a higher pitch to a lower one. It tends to be used for:

- Complete statements
- Commands
- Agreement
- Aggression
- Strong emotion
- Questions not requiring a 'yes' or 'no' answer
- End of breath-groups.

Try these examples using a Falling Tune:
- We are fortunate to have John Smith spending the day with us.
- Put that on the table.
- I agree with your opinion.

Rising Tune. This is also a pattern of descending stressed syllables, but there is a rise of pitch on the last syllable. It tends to be used for:

- Doubt
- Anxiety
- Surprise
- Pleading
- Threats
- Incomplete statements
- Questions requiring a 'yes' or 'no' answer
- The end of a single sense-group within a larger breath-group.

Try these examples using a Rising Tune:
- I'm not too sure about that one.
- Please don't leave me now.
- Would you like to come to the football match?

Inflection reflects our personality, our thoughts and our feelings. Flexible use of inflection will therefore reveal subtle changes in our moods. Use of inflection must be unconscious or speech becomes stilted. The speaker should focus on communicating meaning and mood to avoid artificiality.

(g) Tone colour. Tone colour refers to the variation of 'light' and 'shade' in the voice. It is the result of various tensions and relaxations in the resonators and other associated muscles but is prompted by the imagination and emotion. The quality of tone therefore alters according to the feelings, which helps the listener to recognise the mood of the speaker regardless of the words spoken.

In performance, the tone colour should reflect the mood of the prose or verse, but this must be sincerely imagined or it will sound false.

(h) Intensity. Fluctuations in intensity indicate tension and relaxation according to the prevailing mood. A performer should avoid giving a whole performance at a high pitch of intensity as it is too tiring for both the performer and audience and the value of contrast and sincerity would be lost.

> Now think about when and why you use these features in the performance of your verse and prose. Be prepared to give the examiner specific examples.

GRADE EIGHT – GOLD MEDAL

Questions will be based on the following:

- *A detailed understanding of the content of the chosen selections.*
- *Metre and rhythm (iambic, anapaestic, trochaic, dactylic and spondaic rhythms). Definitions must be illustrated with examples from the chosen pieces where possible.*
- *The writers' key biographical details and the context of their writing.*

The learner must be prepared to discuss with the examiner any aspect of theory specified for previous grades.

A detailed understanding

This requires an in-depth comprehension of the chosen selections, together with the ability to concisely discuss them in detail.

Versification

Versification is the art of making verses or the theory of the phonetic structure of verse. In the English language the basic system of versification is known as accentual-syllabic. This describes the pattern made between the number of syllables in the line of verse and the accents placed on them. In most English poetry the verse structure is created in this way, by balancing the fixed or varying numbers of syllables in a line with the constant alternation of accented and unaccented syllables in definite, recurring sequences.

Metre and rhythm

English speech rhythm is formed by a combination of weak and strong stresses. English verse rhythm depends upon the arrangement of these stresses into patterns. When that pattern is regular and repeated it is called **metre**.

One bar or unit of a metrical form is called a **foot**, derived from dancing in Ancient Greece when the foot was raised and set down on the stressed beat of a musical bar.

A metric line is named according to the number of feet:

Monometer	=	one foot to a line
Dimeter	=	two feet to a line
Trimeter	=	three feet to a line
Tetrameter	=	four feet to a line
Pentameter	=	five feet to a line
Hexameter	=	six feet to a line
Heptameter	=	seven feet to a line
Octometer	=	eight feet to a line

A metric line is also named according to the type of **rhythm** within the unit or bar. In English verse there are two main types: Rising Rhythm and Falling Rhythm.

(a) Rising Rhythm

- **Iambus (an iambic foot).** An iambic foot consists of an unstressed followed by a stressed syllable.

  weak <u>strong</u> | weak <u>strong</u> | weak <u>strong</u> | weak <u>strong</u> | weak <u>strong</u> | (iambic pentameter)

  de <u>dum</u> | de <u>dum</u> | de <u>dum</u> | de <u>dum</u> | de <u>dum</u> | (iambic pentameter)

  It comes from the Greek word meaning 'to hurl' or 'to throw', used when writers of satire hurled their verse, like a weapon, at their enemies. The rhythm resembles the beating of a human heart and is very close to natural speech patterns. Although we may not be aware of it, everyday conversation frequently falls into an iambic rhythm.

I hope you take the book with you to school.
I <u>hope</u> | you <u>take</u> | the <u>book</u> | with <u>you</u> | to <u>school</u>

The ticket isn't valid for today.
The <u>tick</u> | et <u>is</u> | n't <u>val</u> | id <u>for</u> | to<u>day</u>

This is one reason why Elizabethan dramatists, who were heavily influenced by the metrical forms adopted by the Greek and Latin poets of antiquity, were attracted to it. The forward drive of the iambus also makes it ideal for ongoing narrative.

Romeo speaks in iambic pentameter as he waits below Juliet's window in *Romeo and Juliet.*

But soft! What light through yonder window breaks?
But <u>soft!</u> | What <u>light</u> | through <u>yon</u> | der <u>win</u> | dow <u>breaks?</u>

Notice how the metrical structure of the line gives emphasis to the words 'soft', 'light' and 'breaks'.

- **Anapaest (an anapaestic foot).** An anapaestic foot consists of two unstressed syllables followed by a stressed syllable.

  de de <u>dum</u> | de de <u>dum</u> | de de <u>dum</u> | de de <u>dum</u> | de de <u>dum</u>

  This creates a rapid effect, driving the line of the verse forward, which mirrors the movement in Lord Byron's *The Destruction of Sennacherib.*

  The Assyrian came down like the wolf on the fold;

And his cohorts were gleaming in purple and gold:

The A<u>ssyr</u> | ian came <u>down</u> | like the <u>wolf</u> | on the <u>fold</u>;
And his <u>co</u> | horts were <u>gleam</u> | ing in <u>pur</u> | ple and <u>gold</u>:

(b) Falling Rhythm

- **Trochee (a trochaic foot).** A trochaic foot consists of a stressed syllable followed by an unstressed syllable.

<u>dum</u> de | <u>dum</u> de | <u>dum</u> de | <u>dum</u> de | <u>dum</u> de

<u>Nev</u>er | <u>Nev</u>er | <u>Nev</u>er | <u>Nev</u>er | <u>Nev</u>er

King Lear's response upon discovering his daughter Cordelia dead, is captured in the mournful, falling tone of the metre. Shakespeare often uses a trochee at the start of an iambic line, which emphasises the meaning of the first word, as in *Sonnet 27*, for example:

Weary with toil, I haste me to my bed,
<u>Wear</u>y | with <u>toil</u>, | I <u>haste</u> | me <u>to</u> | my <u>bed</u>,

- **Dactyl (a dactylic foot).** A dactylic foot consists of a stressed syllable followed by two unstressed syllables.

<u>dum</u> de de | <u>dum</u> de de | <u>dum</u> de de | <u>dum</u> de de | <u>dum</u> de de

In the following line from *Hamlet* the metre places stress on the word 'that', highlighting the reflective nature of the speech and drawing our attention to the 'question'. The use of two lighter syllables in the fourth foot rapidly moves the line forward to 'question'.

To be, or not to be, that is the question
To <u>be</u>, | or <u>not</u> | to <u>be</u>, | <u>that</u> is the | <u>quest</u>ion

(c) Other rhythms.

- **Spondee (a spondaic foot).** A spondaic foot consists of two successive syllables with equal weight.

  | <u>dum</u> <u>dum</u> |

  It is usually used in the middle or end of a line for extra emphasis. An example can be found in *The Rime of the Ancient Mariner* by Samuel Taylor Coleridge.

  Alone, alone, <u>all</u>, <u>all</u> alone,
  Alone on a wide, wide sea!

(d) Examples. Examples of these feet in English prosody:

- Iambus – a<u>way</u>
- Anapaest – in com<u>plete</u>
- Trochee – <u>du</u>ty
- Dactyl – <u>me</u>rrily
- Spondee – <u>old</u> <u>time</u>

(e) Blending of rhythms. A succession of lines consisting of the same kind of metrical rhythm can be monotonous. Many poets therefore combine different rhythms to create interest. Sometimes a poem can pass from rising to falling rhythm and back again. A change in rhythm can bring a change in the meaning or mood; equally, a change in the meaning or mood can bring a change in the rhythm.

(f) Scansion. To scan a piece of verse is to go through it line by line, analysing the number of feet and marking the weak and strong stresses. Whilst it is not necessary to scan poems or speeches in detail, it is absolutely imperative that you have a firm grasp of the ways in which poetic structure links with thought and emotion. An understanding of metrical patterning can often provide the key to the meaning of a passage that might at first seem difficult to comprehend. If you know where the stresses fall in a given speech you will find it easier to understand and communicate the sense of the writing.

It is important that the rules of poetic form are not applied to the exclusion of thought and emotion. Working with the rhythm and metre must be connected to feeling and impulse. Over-emphasis of the metre can be to the detriment of the mood and the poet's intention.

Key biographical details

This section includes an overview of the key aspects of the writers' background together with an appreciation of the context of their writing. Students should also be aware of the writers' other works.

The following pages provide information on the writers listed in the syllabus.

Jane Austen (1775 – 1817)

"I do not want people to be agreeable, as it saves me the trouble of liking them."

Due to the modern media of films and television Jane Austen is known as 'a great English writer' although during her lifetime her works were not greatly recognized. Her books are widely read and she is one of the most popular writers in English Literature. In her lifetime four major novels were published, *Sense and Sensibility* (1811), *Pride and Prejudice* (1813), *Mansfield Park* (1814), and *Emma* (1815). Two additional novels were published after her death in 1817: *Northanger Abbey* and *Persuasion*. She began a third entitled *Sanditon*, but she died before completing it.

Jane was born in England in 1775 into a large family (of six brothers and one sister) at Steventon Rectory. In 1783 she and her sister were sent to Oxford, according to family tradition, to be educated by Mrs Crawley. They moved with her to Southampton. Whilst there both girls contracted typhus so were forced to return home where they were educated before going to boarding school in Oxford. By December 1786 the two girls had to return home as their father, Reverend Austen, could not afford to send both daughters to school. From that date Jane lived at home completing her education by reading her father's books from his extensive library. She was encouraged by him to write, and he provided both sisters with expensive paper and other materials. The support from her family was critical to her growth as a professional writer.

During this period, private theatricals became a very important part of Jane's life. From the age of seven to thirteen her family and close friends gave performances of several plays, including Richard Sheridan's *The Rivals*. These are said to have influenced Jane, cultivating her gift for comedy and satire. She began writing at an early age. These juvenilia were often parodies of the excesses of contemporary fiction, such as gothic romances. Among these, *Love and Friendship* was written when she was 14, *A History of England (by a partial, ignorant and prejudiced historian)* at 15 and *A Collection of Letters* at 16.

Through adulthood she continued to live with her parents, pursuing the usual duties of a young woman of her social standing: practising the pianoforte, supervising the servants, dressmaking and generally socializing. Jane never married but she spent a considerable time with the nephew of a neighbour, Tom Lefroy. The Lefroy family intervened and sent him away. In 1802 she received and accepted a proposal from Harris Bigg-Wither, 'a large plain-looking man with a stutter'. The next morning Jane realised her mistake and withdrew her acceptance.

Between 1793 and 1795 Jane wrote a short epistolary entitled *Lady Susan*. This was often described as her most sophisticated work. Claire Tomalin wrote: 'Told in letters, it is as neatly plotted as a play and as cynical in tone as any of the most outrageous of the restoration dramatists who may have provided some of her inspiration… It stands alone in Austen's work as a study of an adult woman whose intelligence and force of character are greater than those of anyone she encounters.' After completing *Lady Susan* she attempted her first full length novel, *Eleanor and Marianne*. Her sister recalled it being read to the family before 1796. There are no surviving manuscripts to indicate whether this was part of the original draft for *Sense and Sensibility*, but this is likely.

In 1796, at the age of twenty-one, Jane completed her second novel, *First Impressions* (later known as *Pride and Prejudice*), only to have it turned down by the publisher. In 1798 she began writing her third novel entitled *Susan*, later known as *Northanger Abbey*.

In 1800 her father retired to Bath, much to Jane's distress, taking the family with him. In 1804, whilst living there, Jane began a new novel, *The Watsons*. However she did not complete the story as the central figure was an invalid clergyman with four dependant unmarried daughters, and it was said to be too autobiographical. The novel was described by Sutherland as 'a study in the harsh economic realities of dependent women's lives.' Her father died in January 1805.

Jane, her mother and her sister were left impoverished and were financially supported by her brothers. In 1809 they eventually moved to a large cottage in the village of Chawton, near Alton. Anna, Jane's niece, described their life there as 'very quiet according to our ideas, but they were great readers. They occupied themselves by working with the poor and teaching some children to read or to write.' In this quiet environment Jane once again became a productive writer. She was content to live within the confines of her family to whom – particularly her sister Cassandra – she was devoted.

Four of her novels were successfully published whilst at Chawton: *Sense and Sensibility, Pride and Prejudice, Mansfield Park*, and *Emma*. Jane became ill in 1816, but she completed her first draft of *Persuasion*. Her health deteriorated throughout the year and she died in 1817.

The epitaph composed by her brothers praised 'the extraordinary endowments of her mind.' Sir Walter Scott, a novelist, applauded her realism and 'that exquisite touch which renders ordinary common-place things and characters interesting'. Richard Whately commented on the 'dramatic quality of her narrative' and likened her to Homer and Shakespeare. The Prince Regent kept a set of her novels at each of his residences.

The revisionists, F R Leavis and Ian Watts, stated that Jane was one of the great writers of English fiction. They held that 'she combined qualities of interiority and irony, realism and satire to form an author superior to both.'

She had a few critics too. Charlotte Brönte, Elizabeth Barrett Browning and D H Lawrence found her limitations too great, restricting her concerns to such a small section of society. However, for the majority of her readers it is such detailed focus that makes her unique.

She wrote about what was familiar to her – the provincial middle-class life of Regency England; of family and human affairs (public events are seldom mentioned) – and of this her knowledge was deep and true. Her witty observations (particularly of female characters) and delicate irony enriched the novels with subtle humour. The light wit became sharper in the later novels, where follies and vanities were more keenly scrutinised. Her plots were carefully constructed and she had a gift for dialogue.

Julian Barnes (1946 – present)

"Love is just a system for getting someone to call you darling after sex."

Julian Patrick Barnes was born in Leicester, England. He has written novels, books of short stories, essays, a collection of writings about cookery and translations of both French and German books. His writing earned him critical acclaim and many awards. He was shortlisted three times for the Man Booker Prize: in 1984, 1998 and 2005. He deals with themes of history, reality, truth and love.

After school he studied at Magdalen College, Oxford, where he graduated in modern languages. He then worked as a lexicographer for the Oxford English Dictionary. After this he worked as a reviewer and literary editor, then for seven years as a television critic. He now writes full-time and over the space of twenty years has produced slightly more than twenty books, mostly novels. Under the pseudonym of Dan Kavanagh he has also published four crime novels featuring the bi-sexual private eye, Duffy.

Metroland (1980), his first novel, was published when he was 34. It is a short, semi-autobiographical story of a young student from London escaping suburbia by travelling to Paris (and later returning). It dealt with themes of idealism and sexual fidelity. Two years later he released his second novel, *Before She Met Me,* which is altogether darker. It was a story of revenge by a jealous historian who became obsessed by his wife's past.

Flaubert's Parrot (1984) was a fragmentary biographical narrative of an elderly doctor who became obsessed with the life of the great French novelist Gustave Flaubert. The novel was published to great acclaim, especially in France, and it was Barnes' breakthrough novel. It was nominated for the Man Booker Prize.

Staring at the Sun (1986) was an ambitious novel about a woman growing to maturity in post-war England who considers love, truth and mortality. *A History of the World in 10 1/2 Chapters* (1989) was a non-linear novel which used a variety of writing styles to question how we perceive history, art and religion and the changeability of human knowledge. *Talking it Over* (1991) explored a contemporary love triangle, in which the three characters considered the same events and took turns to lead the narrative. The sequel *Love, Etc.* (2000) picked up the story ten years later.

Barnes has a strong interest in French culture. *Cross Channel* (1996) was a collection of ten stories concerning Britain's relationship with France. *Something to Declare* (2002) was a collection of essays on French subjects.

His second nomination for a Booker Prize came with a satire of British 'theme-park' culture titled *England, England*, published in 1998.

His third nomination was for a detailed story titled *Arthur and George* (2005). It was set in late-Victorian Britain and was the true story of the intersection of two lives: one an internationally famous author, and the other, an obscure country lawyer. It explores themes of love, longing, loss, victimisation and man's inhumanity to man. In the story we learn of another side to the famous author Sir Arthur Conan Doyle. The creator of Sherlock Holmes actually tried to kill his character off but was forced to resurrect him because of the outcry of his fans. Doyle also married, and fathered two children, but his wife became an invalid due to consumption and he fell madly in love (for the first time) with another woman. Although the relationship was kept discreet and chaste, he was plagued by guilt. Just like his fictional character Sherlock Holmes, Doyle threw himself into the challenge of fighting injustice, clearing the name of a timid lawyer who had been victimised.

The Lemon Table (2004) was a collection of short fiction in which the characters were linked by their nearness to old age and death. This preoccupation with death was continued in his most recent book, *Nothing to be Frightened Of* (2008), which was a family memoir, an exchange with his brother (Jonathan Barnes is a philosopher specializing in Ancient Philosophy), a meditation on mortality, a celebration of art, an argument about God and a homage to the French writer Jules Renard.

His many awards include the Somerset Maugham Award, Geoffrey Faber Memorial Prize, the Prix Médicis and the Prix Femina, E M Forster Award (American Academy and Institute of Arts and Letters), Gutenberg Prize, Grinzane Cavour Prize (Italy), the Shakespeare Prize (FVS Foundation), the Austrian State Prize for European Literature and the Order of Arts and Literature of France.

He lives in London and lived together with his wife, the literary agent Pat Kavanagh, until her death in 2008. He writes using an old electric typewriter in a bright yellow writing room which helps him to believe that the sun is still shining.

John Berendt (1939 – present)

"Nothing can be said, including this statement, that has not been said before."

John Berendt is best known for his book, *Midnight in the Garden of Good and Evil*, which was a finalist for the 1995 Pulitzer Prize in General Non-fiction. It chronicled the real-life events surrounding a murder trial in Savannah, Georgia (USA). It was written with a Southern Gothic tone and it revealed the cultural character of the American South. Although it read like a novel, it was based on real events and was classified as a nonfiction book.

Berendt first travelled to Savannah in the early 1980s, when he realized that he could fly there for a three-day weekend for the price of 'a paillard of veal served on a bed of wilted radicchio' in one of New York's trendier restaurants. He eventually moved to Savannah and lived there for five years so that he could discover the true essence of the people. He loved the slow-moving lifestyle there.

When he submitted the manuscript of *Midnight in the Garden of Good and Evil* to his literary agent she rejected it. Undaunted, he sent it to another agent, and within days had offers from five publishing houses. The book was published in 1994 and it became an overnight success. It spent over four years on the New York Times bestseller list, largely due to the way the book brought the dark mystique of Savannah so startlingly to life. It was also made into a film directed by Clint Eastwood, although Berendt had no control over changes made to the story. In an interview, he thanked Clint Eastwood, in a humorous manner, 'for taking time from his busy schedule to make a ten million dollar commercial for my book'.

John Berendt has spent his life working with words. He worked in a bookstore when he was fourteen years old. Both of his parents were writers. He grew up in Syracuse (New York State, USA) went to Harvard University to study English, then moved to New York City to be a journalist. From 1961 to 1969 he worked as associate editor of Esquire Magazine (a men's magazine with a strong literary tradition). From 1977 to 1979 he spent two years as the editor of the New York Magazine (a weekly lifestyle magazine that comments on culture and politics) before returning to Esquire as a columnist from 1982 to 1994.

The great success of his first book allowed him the better part of a decade to figure out what to write next. He looked into several stories that came his way but they weren't satisfying, so he took a methodical approach and considered what worked in the first book. Generally speaking it was place, characters and the story. He asked himself what other place was as magical as Savannah but very different. This led him to travel to Venice. By sheer chance a famous and iconic opera house, *The Fenice*, burned down three days before he arrived, apparently due to a small-time arson attempt that had gone horribly wrong. The prosecution became embroiled in ridiculous bureaucratic turmoil and corruption. He had his story – *The City of Falling Angels* (published in 2005).

He took his time researching Venice, exploring the city, going to dinner with people, reading newspapers and absorbing the culture. Berendt felt it was important to find stories that buttressed the main narrative, so that what emerged was not just a story about the fire, but a contemporary portrait of Venice. He included a host of saints, sinners, rogues and fools whose interwoven stories painted a colourful picture of Venetian life.

Among those interviewed was Archimede Seguso, a renowned Venetian glassblower who lived directly behind the burnt opera house and who was deeply affected by the loss. The book included the stories of American and English expatriates who went to live in Venice, and as it inquired into the nature of life in the museum-city of Venice, it gradually revealed the truth about the fire and the locals' reaction to it. With *The Fenice* gone, Venice had no major stage for the performing arts, and Berendt used the fact to question whether Venice was a living or dead city. It once had twelve opera houses and now it had none. Did it live on only through tourists as a cultural theme-park? Or did it still have a life of its own?

The City of Falling Angels also rose to number one on the New York Times bestseller list.

Laurence Binyon (1869 – 1943)

"They shall grow not old, as we that are left grow old: Age shall not weary them, nor the years condemn…"

Robert Laurence Binyon was born in Lancaster, England. He was primarily a poet but also produced many works as an art critic.

His most famous poem, *For the Fallen*, is used in worldwide Remembrance services to mark the anniversary of the end of the First World War. The chorus is:

They shall grow not old, as we that are left grow old:
Age shall not weary them, nor the years condemn.
At the going down of the sun and in the morning
We will remember them. We will remember them."

The poem adorns numerous war memorials.

His parents were Quakers (a non-heirarchical Christian peace church). Binyon was educated at St Paul's School and Trinity College, Oxford. He won the Newdigate Prize for a poem whilst at Oxford.

After graduation in 1893, he worked at the Department of Printed Books in the British Museum, where he produced biographies, books and catalogues. In 1904 he married fellow historian Cicely Margaret Powell, and they had three daughters who all grew up to be artists (the first an illustrator, the second a writer, the third a calligrapher and art scholar).

He was too old to enlist in the First World War, but he went to the Western Front in 1916 to work for the Red Cross as a medical orderly. He wrote about his experiences in his autobiographical book *For Dauntless France* (1918). He was a scholar of both East and West – he wrote many books on William Blake and numerous others concerning Oriental Art.

From the age of 25 he produced a regular poetry book approximately every three years, but his most notable was the two volume *Collected Poems* published in 1931. In 1933 he was appointed as a professor of poetry at Harvard and the next year he resigned from the British Museum and moved to the English countryside. He continued working as an academic and poet.

In 1940 he was appointed Professor of English Literature at the University of Athens. He worked there until forced to leave before the German invasion of Greece in April 1941.

War is a common theme of his poetry. *For the Fallen* has played its part in developing a mystical belief that there was something very special about those young men who died in the Great War – that they were the finest of their generation. This was a sentiment that became very common in post-war writing. There was a belief that the Great War had swept away all that was noble and great and replaced it with drabness and strife, and Binyon's poetry captured that disillusionment well.

> And now I hear everywhere sound of battle
> The seekers after destruction, there is no refuge
> Death, death, death on the earth, in the sea, in the air
> Yet oh, it is a single soul always in the midst
> Each is a single soul.
> O it cannot be, yet it is…
> *[from Winter Sunrise]*

He wrote in a gothic style that often featured ruins, death, fires, spirits and a melancholic longing for nature:

But O divine diversity of creatures,
Where are you? Not here amid man's contrivings;
[from Ezekiel]

He was also concerned with the loss of humanity:
Truth, justice, love, beauty, the human smile,
All flung to the flames!
[from Beautiful, Wearied Head]

He was not limited to poetry or scholarly works; he also completed six stage plays, an acclaimed translation of Dante's *Divine Comedy* and in his final years he was working on an Arthurian trilogy – the first part of which was published after his death as *The Madness of Merlin* (1947).

Binyon was among sixteen Great War Poets commemorated on a slate stone unveiled in Westminster Abbey in 1985.

John Donne (1572 – 1631)
"Any man's death diminishes me, because I am involved in Mankind; And therefore never send to know for whom the bell tolls; it tolls for thee."

His name is usually pronounced (and was frequently spelt) Dunne. John Donne was born in London to Roman Catholic parents, the third of six children. His father, John, was of Welsh descent, a warden of the Ironmongers' Company, and his mother, Elizabeth, was the daughter of John Haywood (the playwright) and the great niece of the martyr Thomas More. This tradition of martyrdom would continue among Donne's relatives, many of whom were executed or exiled for religious reasons.

Despite the obvious dangers of persecution for religious commitment, Donne's family sent him to be educated by the Jesuits. He studied at both Oxford and Cambridge but was unable to obtain a Degree from either university as he refused to take the Oath of Supremacy required of graduates. His brother Henry was also a university student before being arrested in 1593 for harbouring a Catholic priest. Henry died in prison of bubonic plague which led John to begin questioning his Catholic faith.

After University he was accepted as a law student at Lincoln's Inn, one of the Inns of Court in London, before embarking with the Earl of Essex and Sir Walter Raleigh to fight the Spanish at Cadiz in 1591. His adventuring extended to the Azores in 1597 where he witnessed the loss of the Spanish flagship, San Felipe, and her crew. These experiences were reflected in his early poems *The Storm* and *The Calm*.

By the age of twenty-five he was ready to embark on a Diplomatic career and was appointed chief secretary to Sir Thomas Egerton, Lord Keeper of the Great Seal. He was established at Egerton's London Home in Whitehall, the centre of society in England. During the next four years he fell in love with Sir Thomas's niece Anne More, and they were married secretly in 1601 against the wishes of both Egerton and Anne's father. This ended Donne's diplomatic career and he was put in the Fleet Prison together with the priest who married them, and the witness to the wedding. He was quickly released when the marriage was proved valid, but it was not until 1609 that Donne was reconciled with his father-in-law and received his wife's dowry.

Donne and his wife retired to Pyrton in Surrey where he barely made a living as a lawyer, depending heavily on Sir Francis Wolly, his wife's cousin, to house him and his quickly growing family. In all, Anne had eleven children; nine survived. John and Anne's deep affection endured the sixteen years of their marriage until Anne died in childbirth. The passionate love poems John wrote were most likely to have been the reflection of their relationship. He mourned her deeply when she died and never remarried. This was unusual for the time, especially as he had a large family to raise. After Anne's death he wrote the *17th Holy Sonnet*.

He was elected as a member of parliament for Brackley in 1602 but it was not a paid position and Donne struggled to provide for his family, relying on rich friends. He found patronage in Sir Robert Drury in 1610 and it was for him that he wrote the two Anniversaries *An Anatomy of the World* in 1611 and *Of the Progress of the Soul* in 1612.

It is uncertain exactly why Donne left the Catholic Church. He was certainly in communication with King James The First of England in 1610 and 1611 as he wrote two anti-Catholic polemics, *Pseudo Martyr* and *Ignatius his Conclave*. Although James admired Donne's work, he refused to re-instate him in court and urged him to take holy orders. He finally acceded to the King's wishes and was ordained into the Church of England in 1615, becoming the Royal Chaplain in the same year and Reader of Divinity at Lincoln's Inn in 1616.

In 1621 Donne was made Dean of St Paul's, a well-paid, leading position which he held until his death. In 1623 he suffered a near fatal illness and during his convalescence wrote a series of prayers and meditations. These concerned health, pain and sickness, and were published in a book entitled *Devotions upon Emergent Occasions*. They are memorable for the phrases 'for whom the bell tolls' and 'no man is an island'. He proved an impressive, eloquent preacher, his sermons are some of the most moving prose of the period. One-hundred-and-sixty of his sermons survive, many delivered to King Charles the First at the Palace of Whitehall.

His verse is distinguished by wit, profundity of thought, passion and subtlety. He was the greatest of the Puritan poets (better known as the 'Metaphysical Poets') in which passion is interwoven with reasoning. He asserted that anything could be a fit subject for poetry if realistically and intellectually treated.

Among his more important poems is the satirical *Progresse of the Soule* begun in 1601 but never finished, in which he traces the migration of the Soul of Eve's apple through the bodies of various heretics. His best known poems are some of the miscellaneous ones, like *The Ecstasi, Hymn to God the Father, The Good-Morrow, Death be not Proud* and *Go and Catch a Falling Star*.

His verse is characterised by the use of the 'conceit', a device whereby an idea is expressed in unusual or unexpected terms. Clever use of metaphors and similes arrest attention by painting startling word pictures. This technique is vividly illustrated in *The Flea*, where Donne displays all his wit and ingenuity. Striving to move away from classical verse forms and regular rhythms, his poetic metre was often jagged and he sought out the strongest images, combining ideas which no one had yet seen together.

Considering his religious calling, it is perhaps surprising to discover the sensual nature of many of his poems. He is a lover who often explores his emotions in philosophical or scientific terms.

His work had enormous influence on literature and language, not confined to his contemporary followers but spanning centuries to colour the work of Coleridge, Browning and the twentieth century T S Eliot. Thomas Carew described him as 'a king who ruled as he thought fit, the universal monarchy of wit'. A fitting epitaph. John Donne is buried in St Paul's Cathedral.

Lawrence Durrell (1912 – 1990)

"A city becomes a world when one loves one of its inhabitants."

Lawrence George Durrell was born in India (a British Colony at the time) and went to school in Darjeeling until he was twelve when he attended St Edmund's School, Canterbury (in

England). He failed his entrance examinations to Cambridge University, but that didn't stop him from writing poetry.

His first collection, *Quaint Fragments*, was published when he was 19; his first novel, *Pied Piper of Lovers*, when he was 23. He married his first wife Nancy Myers in that same year and moved with his mother and his siblings to the Greek island of Corfu. Lawrence was glad: he didn't like England and he would spend most of his life outside it.

His writer brother, Gerald Durrell, described life there in his book *My Family and Other Animals* (1956). Lawrence made a lifelong friend in doctor and biologist Theodore Stephanides, and a fictionalised account of his life there can be read in his poetic travel book *Prospero's Cell*.

Durrell's next novel, *Panic Spring*, was released under a pseudonym. He joined a few other authors in an attempt to found their own literary movement and improve their publishing opportunities. *The Black Book* was a product of this time – it was a story of a man escaping from the spiritual desolation of England and discovering the warmth and fertility of Greece. It had coarse language and an apocalyptic mood and the style was influenced by his writing mentor Henry Miller. It was published in Paris in 1938 but didn't appear in England until 1973 due to censorship (it contained mild indecency by modern standards).

In 1940 he and his wife had a daughter. After the fall of Greece in the Second World War they escaped to Alexandria in Egypt where Durrell served as a press representative to the British Embassies. He met and fell in love with Eve Cohen, who would become a lead character in his most famous work, *The Alexandria Quartet*. Durrell separated from Nancy in 1942 and later married Eve Cohen.

He worked for the British Council for a while in Argentina, then for some years in Yugoslavia, which gave him material for the novel *White Eagles over Serbia*. But when the next assignment was a choice between Turkey and Russia, he opted to resign and head for his beloved Greece by moving to Cyprus and taking a teaching position. This didn't last. The Cypriot revolution meant foreigners became unwelcome guests and he finally had to move to Provence in France.

Durrell separated from Eve Cohen in 1955. His major work *The Alexandria Quartet* was published in 1957. It was a fascinating story spread across four books. It dealt with the same events leading up to the Second World War from different perspectives. All the characters were bound together in a web of political and sexual intrigue: each novel revealed different aspects of the truth, and each novel climaxed in death. Only in the final book did events advance and reach a conclusion. It was a complex work with a rich and vivid style. It had a broad variety of characters and exotic locations and it shifted from private viewpoints to political observations. The ancient city of Alexandria was itself a central character, with its knowledge, books and stories. It highlighted how the reality of any given situation was profoundly coloured by the perception of whichever character was observing it.

By 1961 he was married again, to Claude-Marie Vincendon, who died of cancer. Durrell's fourth and final marriage in 1973, to Ghislaine de Boysson, lasted only six years.

He wrote *The Revolt of Aphrodite* and then *The Avignon Quintet*, which had many of the motifs and styles of the successful *Alexandria Quartet*. The opening novel, *Monsieur: or, the Prince of Darkness*, received the 1974 James Tait Black Memorial Prize. The middle book, *Constance: or, Solitary Practices* (which portrays France during the German occupation) was nominated for the Booker Prize in 1982.

His last book, *Caesar's Vast Ghost* (1990), was a travel book written from the perspective of an old man reflecting on the Provence region – its landscape, mythologies and people – a celebration of his adoptive home.

He also wrote much poetry, inspired by the Mediterranean landscapes and his experience during his travels. This poetry eventually won him acclaim and a place in the Faber Book of Modern Verse. He wrote four published plays.

Seamus Heaney (1939 – present)
"I rhyme… to see myself, to set the darkness echoing."

For more than forty years Seamus Heaney has provided much pleasure to readers of his own special brand of poetry. His first volume, *Death of a Naturalist,* appeared in 1966 and since then he has produced a collection of poetry approximately every four years.

He was raised on a farm in Derry (Northern Ireland), the eldest of nine children. His father was a farmer and cattle trader and his mother came from a family who worked in a linen mill, so he felt he was influenced by both the cattle-herding Gaelic past and the contrasting culture of the Industrial Revolution. When he was twelve he moved from the rural family life to a school in the city and this transition was to become a recurrent theme in his work, that he calls 'removal from the earth of farm labour to the heaven of education.' Much of his poetry is grounded in the rural setting of County Derry.

He began work as an English school-teacher, then worked as a lecturer before teaching in a teacher training college. He married schoolteacher and writer Marie Devlin in 1965. They were to have three children.

He served on the Republic of Ireland Arts Council for five years. From 1981 he began teaching as visiting professor at Harvard University. The terms of his appointment as Boylston Professor of Rhetoric and Oratory allowed him to spend eight months of the year at home in exchange for a semester of teaching. In 1989 he was appointed as Professor of Poetry at Oxford University (UK) for a five year term – another poet-friendly position which involves appearing at three public lectures a year.

He won the Nobel Prize for Literature in 1995 for what the Nobel committee described as 'works of lyrical beauty and ethical depth, which exalt everyday miracles and the living past'. He was later the President of the British Library Poetry Archive, which collects recordings of poets reading their own work.

The poem *Mid Term Break* recalled the death of his four-year-old brother Christopher in a road accident and the strong effect that this had on him. His insights on family life provide thought-provoking pleasure for many children. His anthologies *The Rattle Bag* and *The School Bag* have both been widely used in UK schools.

Commentators on his style and output have been appreciative, but have noted that he declined to produce work based on 'the troubles' (a period of political and social upheaval in Northern Ireland) when some of his compatriots were writing about the society that was so deeply divided along religious and political lines. When asked about this Heaney is quoted as saying, "I write for myself." His poetry is concerned with profound observations of the details of everyday life rather than political concerns. However, he is proudly Irish and has written: "Be advised, my passport's green. No glass of ours was ever raised, to toast the Queen."

Seamus Heaney has shown great admiration for the work of fellow poets W B Yeats and Ted Hughes. His collection of work *District and Circle* (2006) won the T S Eliot prize for poetry with a cheque for £10,000. The poems in the volume tell of his travels on the London underground system, when he worked in the capital city.

Today his books of poetry make up two thirds of the sales of living poets in the UK. He has had a great impact on the arts and literature. The School of English at Queens University Belfast proudly bears his name, as the Seamus Heaney Centre.

It is impressive that he has written well-regarded plays as well. In 1990 came *The Cure at Troy* based on Sophocles' *Philoctetes*. *The Burial at Thebes* (2003) was also based on a masterpiece by Sophocles, the well known and often performed *Antigone*. It was originally commissioned by Dublin's Abbey Theatre. It has since been revived by Nottingham Playhouse and also presented at the Barbican Theatre in London. Since its origin in ancient Greece the basic storyline has had other interpretations, notably by Jean Anouilh who set it in German occupied France, and by Bertolt Brecht who set a prologue to the play in 1945 in Berlin.

He has also produced ten works of translation, the most notable being the Anglo-Saxon narrative epic *Beowulf* (1999). It came up against J K Rowling's *Harry Potter and the Prisoner of Azkaban* for the Whitbread Book of the Year Award and won by a single vote. The publicity that resulted from the absurd pairing of potential winners brought unprecedented sales for a thousand-year-old tale. In March 2000, *Beowulf* was the best seller in England, due in part to the marvellous language of a retelling that was eerily intriguing.

He is one of those rare writers who is highly rated by critics and academics and yet popular with the common reader as well.

He lives south of Dublin close to the sea where he and his wife have resided for more than thirty years. Here he reflects on people, time, landscape and his childhood in Ulster and incorporates his insights into his poems.

Khaled Hosseini (1965 – present)

"... but better to be hurt by the truth than comforted with a lie."

Khaled Hosseini was born in Kabul, Afghanistan. His father was a diplomat and his mother a history teacher. They moved away from Afghanistan in 1976 due to his father's diplomatic work. After Afghanistan had a violent communist coup with an invasion by the Soviet army, the family sought political asylum in the United States.

Hosseini studied at Santa Clara University where he earned a bachelor's degree in Biology, followed by a Medical Degree from the University of California. He completed his residency and was a practicing intern between 1996 and 2004.

While in medical practice, Hosseini began writing his first novel, *The Kite Runner*, which meant getting up at 4 a.m. to write for two to three hours before going to work. The book was published in 2003 and became an international bestseller. It spent over two years on the New York Times Bestseller List.

The Kite Runner was the story of a young boy, Amir, struggling to establish a closer rapport with his father and coping with the memories of a haunting childhood event. Amir had a close friend who grew up with him in Kabul – Hassan, the son of his father's servant. Hassan was a Hazara, a member of a shunned ethnic minority. When the Soviets invaded and Amir and his father fled the country for a new life in California, Amir thought that he had escaped his past, yet he could not leave the memory of Hassan behind him. The novel explored themes of betrayal, the price of loyalty, and the ethnic tensions between the Hazara and Pashtun in Afghanistan. Written against a history from the final days of the monarchy until the collapse of the Taliban regime, it described the rich culture and beauty of a land in the process of being destroyed. Ultimately, it was a novel about seeking redemption.

The Kite Runner was a word-of-mouth success that took some time to build a sales momentum and eventually reached a turning point. Hosseini continued working as an intern even as sales of *The Kite Runner* soared to over eighteen million copies worldwide. He was reluctant to give up the security of a job and still found it hard to believe that his writing career would last. He had no intention of quitting medicine and becoming a writer, but the demands of both careers became too heavy. He was quoted as saying, "When my patients would come in to visit me, more out of a sense of getting a book signed than getting their diabetes treated, I started to see the writing on the wall." It was time to become a full-time writer.

His second novel, *A Thousand Splendid Suns*, was published in 2007 and also reached number one on the New York Times Bestseller List. Whereas *The Kite Runner* dealt with brotherhood and fatherhood and the lives of men, *A Thousand Splendid Suns* addresses the issues pertaining to women.

The two main female characters in *A Thousand Splendid Suns* were inspired by his collective sense of what women in Afghanistan went through, particularly since the withdrawal of the Soviets and the breakout of anarchy, extremism and criminality. It was a disturbing story of two women victims of the wrath of men, an insight into the madness and suffering of Afghanistan and a study of love and self-sacrifice in a modern Afghan family.

When Hosseini travelled to Afghanistan in 2003 he accumulated a diverse repertoire of vivid eyewitness accounts and heartbreaking stories. At the time he didn't realise he was getting inspiration for a book – he just wanted to learn about the country as he had been out of Afghanistan for twenty-three years. He spoke to a lot of boys and women in the street, learning about what they had gone through. Thinking about these women, he formed the two main characters in the novel. One is a poor villager who lives in a remote area, the other a smart, educated daughter of a schoolteacher who has high aspirations for her future. Circumstance and tragedy brings them together and they grow to be close friends. The book was about family, friendship, and the longing for acceptance against the background of the upheavals in Afghanistan.

"There's been so much written about Afghanistan, but so little about the inner life of the people living in those situations," said Hosseini in an interview. Hosseini hopes that after reading *A Thousand Splendid Suns* people will have more empathy for the plight of the Afghan people, particularly Afghan women who, in his opinion, have suffered the most.

Hosseini's own experience of Afghanistan was quite different to the Afghanistan of his books. He has nothing but fond memories of his upbringing in Kabul, where he had a very rich social life, being part of a large extended family. It was a peaceful era, before the Soviet invasion. Life revolved around being with people. Kabul was a thriving cosmopolitan city with an active intellectual life, very different to the image of Kabul today.

Even back in those days he'd begun to write stories. He was raised in a very literate family: his parents could recite poetry and there were lots of books around the house. He began writing short stories and plays that were produced for gatherings of friends and family. Reading and writing have always been a major part of his life and he considered himself a writer long before he chose to study medicine. Amongst his many writing influences he lists Persian poetry and John Steinbeck's *The Grapes of Wrath*.

In 2006 he was named a goodwill envoy to United Nations High Commissioner for Refugees, which is a United Nations agency mandated to protect and support refugees and assist in their voluntary repatriation, local integration or resettlement.

Rudyard Kipling (1865 – 1936)

"All the people like us are We, and everyone else is They."

Although he has fallen out of critical favour in recent years for his jingoism, his best poetry and prose deserve to be seriously considered. His poem *If* was a classic and many of his very rhythmic ditties were very speakable. As a novelist he will be remembered for his children's classics, *The Jungle Book, Kim* and *Just So Stories*, but to get the flavour of his adventure stories for adults, try *The Man Who Would Be King*. This is very representative of a genre which includes writers like H Rider Haggard (*King Solomon's Mines, She*) and Sir Arthur Conan Doyle (*The Lost World, Sherlock Holmes*).

Joseph Rudyard Kipling was born in 1865 in Bombay, India at the time of the Raj (the British rule of the Indian Subcontinent, which lasted from 1858–1947). His father, Lockwood Kipling, studied art and sculpture in London and helped in building the Victoria and Albert Museum. He then moved to Staffordshire to design pottery and met his future wife in a factory. They became engaged by the shore of Rudyard Lake Reservoir near Stoke on Trent. Immediately after their marriage in 1865, they left for India where Lockwood Kipling had been appointed first Principal at the new Art and Industry School in Bombay.

Rudyard was the eldest of two children and for six years spoke Hindustani as a second language. In 1871 Rudyard and his sister Alice were sent to England, to avoid the impact of the Indian climate on their health. They were taken as boarders by the Holloway family in Southsea (Portsmouth). This became a bitter experience for Rudyard, which he recounted in his first novel *The Light that Failed* (1890) and in the short story *Baa Baa Black Sheep* (1898).

He was removed and sent to a school to prepare boys for the armed forces. His schoolboy tales were recalled in the novel *Stalky & Co* (1899). At school he wrote verse and became editor of the school magazine. His headmaster advised Rudyard's parents that he lacked the academic ability for Oxford and suggested a profession in literature.

Lockwood Kipling had moved to Lahore (now in Pakistan) and obtained a job for his son on the Lahore Civil & Military Gazette. Rudyard returned to India just before his seventeenth birthday to begin work as a journalist (1882–1889). These years provided virtually all the material for his early poems and books. His first collection of verse *Departmental Ditties* was published in 1886 and was well received in England. In the space of less than a year, thirty-nine of his short stories appeared in the Gazette. These formed his first prose collection *Plain Tales from the Hills*, published a month after his twenty-second birthday.

He was transferred to a much larger newspaper in Allahabad. His writing output remained prolific and six other prose collections including *Wee Willie Winkie* were published in 1988. This included some stories about children. He now had over seventy published stories. Most of these and his early poems had originally been printed in newspapers or for the Indian Railway Library.

Kipling left India in March 1889 to return to England, where his stories had become hugely popular. He travelled extensively through the Far East, Japan, United States and Canada. He was welcomed into the London literary world. He had a huge success with *Barrack Room Ballads* (1892).

In London he met and became engaged to Caroline (Carrie) Balestier, an American and sister of his American agent. They married in 1892. They set out for a trip around the world, but unfortunately their savings failed in Japan and they had to return to Carrie's home in Vermont, where their three children were born. Kipling wrote the two *Jungle Books* (1894/5) and *Captain Courageous* (1897). The latter book reflected his feelings of affection and irritation about America.

The family returned to England in 1896 and Kipling wrote

Stalky & Co. and *Just So Stories*. He had started these in America to amuse his daughter Josephine. Early in 1898 the family travelled to South Africa for a winter holiday, which was to become an annual tradition. They returned to America for a visit in 1899, but unfortunately Josephine developed pneumonia shortly after arriving in New York and died.

Kipling completed *Kim* (1901), which he had begun writing in 1892. It is generally considered to be his finest novel describing the people, customs and scenes of India at the time of the Raj and British Imperialism.

Although he continued to travel extensively, Kipling bought a house in East Sussex (UK) which inspired two poetry and short story collections – *Puck of Pook's Hill* (1906) and *Rewards and Fairies* (1910). The second contained his most famous poem, *If*, which was voted Britain's favourite poem in a 1995 BBC opinion poll.

It is believed that Kipling declined the position of British Poet Laureate, although he was regarded as the People's Laureate. He also declined a knighthood and the Order of Merit. He was, however, the first English writer to receive the Nobel Prize for Literature, in 1907.

Kipling applied his influence to get his son John a commission in the Irish Guards, but tragedy struck when John was killed during the Battle of Loos (in 1915 during World War One). His feelings of guilt made him join the Imperial War Graves Commission, which look after the garden-like war graves found around the world. Also in response, he wrote a two volume history of the Irish Guards (1923) and the short story *The Gardener*.

Kipling kept writing into the 1930s, but with less popular success. His autobiography *Something of Myself* was written in 1935. He died the next year of a haemorrhage from an ulcer. His ashes were buried in Poets' Corner, Westminster Abbey, London. After Carrie Kipling's death in 1939, his house was bequeathed to the National Trust and it became a public museum.

He held the reputation of being the poet of the Empire. His vast and varied output was criticized towards the end of his life as being too patriotic and too much an advocate of British Imperial rule. As the European colonial empires declined in the mid-20th century, his work fell out of fashion. However, his descriptive skills were highly praised. The narration of the early tales of the Raj and his interpretation of how the British Empire was experienced are noted for their realism. His short story *The Man who would be King* (1886) was made into a very successful film in 1975. The *Jungle Book* stories were first filmed by Alexander Korda (1942) and then immortalised by the Disney cartoon musical (1967). The *Just So Stories* have been recreated for the theatre and several of his poems were set to music.

Philip Larkin (1922 – 1985)

"I think writing about unhappiness is probably the source of my popularity, if I have any – after all, most people are unhappy, don't you think?"

Philip Larkin is one of the most widely read of twentieth-century poets. He was born in Coventry, England in 1922. His father was the City Treasurer and had a strong interest in language and literature (he would read Fowler's *Modern English Usage* for pleasure); he was also keen on jazz. His father passed both these interests on to him.

Larkin wrote his first poem at school as a homework assignment when he was sixteen. Until he was twenty-one he suffered with a serious stammer, which undoubtedly contributed to his reputation as a quiet, bookish boy. In 1940 he went to St John's College, Oxford to study English. He failed his Army medical because of poor eye-sight so, unusually for a young man of that time, he had an uninterrupted three years of study and graduated with a First in 1943. While at Oxford he developed his interest in jazz as well as having a wide circle of literary friends, the closest of whom was Kingsley Amis. Their friendship was to be lifelong. Larkin's first published poem appeared in the magazine *The Listener* and several others featured in university magazines.

After graduation Larkin returned to his parents' home briefly. He tried twice, and failed, to get into the Civil Service, and eventually got the job of Librarian. He intended to become a novelist and had already begun work on *Jill*, which drew on his experiences of life in war-time Oxford. Being somewhat isolated away from home and friends did, he later admitted, "create a raw state of mind that was very fruitful." Several of his poems from this period appeared in the anthology *Poetry from Oxford in Wartime* and these were later included in his first individual volume, *The North Ship* (1945). This was followed by *Jill* in 1946 and a year later, *A Girl in Winter*, his second novel in which he made use of his life as a librarian.

In 1947 he moved to Leicester to become Assistant Librarian at University College and began to study part-time for his Library Association Examinations, which he passed in 1949. At this time he met Monica Jones, a lecturer in English, with whom he had a lifelong affair. He began several novels but found himself unable to complete any of them, something his friend Kingsley Amis attributed to Larkin's deep fear of failure.

Larkin made another move in 1950 when he took the post of Sub-Librarian at Queen's University, Belfast, and here he began another fruitful period of writing. In 1951 he had *XX Poems* published privately and three years later his second volume, *The Less Deceived*, which was to form the foundation of his reputation as one of Britain's leading poets.

Larkin's final career move was made in 1955 when he was appointed Librarian at Hull University, where he was to remain for the rest of his life. He confessed to enjoying librarianship and had no desire to become a full-time writer. Hull suited him because he found it "off the beaten track… a lonely place". It was in Hull that he met the other two women with whom he had significant affairs, his fellow librarian, Maeve Brennan, and his secretary Betty Mackereth. But Larkin never married – the ties and demands of a monogamous relationship scared him and interfered with his need for solitude.

It was ten years after the appearance of *The Less Deceived* that Larkin's next volume of poetry was published. *The Whitsun Weddings* cemented his reputation. Some critics saw him as one of the leading figures of 'The Movement', a loosely-knit group of writers who had in common a rejection of modernist ideas and who used plain language and traditional verse forms to appeal to a wider readership.

In 1965 Larkin was awarded the Queen's Gold Medal for Poetry. He rejected the offer to become Poet Laureate after the death of his friend John Betjeman, as this for Larkin would have meant too much time in the public eye.

His last book of verse, *High Windows*, came out in 1974, by which time he was beginning to feel he could no longer write. In an interview in 1982 he commented: "I haven't given poetry up, but I rather think poetry has given me up." He did however continue to be a leading figure on the literary scene.

He produced a book of miscellaneous prose writings, *Required Writing*, in 1983 which won the W H Smith Literary Award. He also served as chairman of the judges for the Booker Prize, was a member of the literary panel of the Arts Council, and edited the popular Oxford Book of Twentieth Century Verse. He died of cancer in 1985, having been elected a Companion of Honour earlier in the year.

In spite of Larkin's rather dour public persona and his nick-name, 'The Hermit of Hull', his poetry has proved remarkably popular. His writing was usually direct and dealt with ordinary characters in everyday situations, often in an urban setting. *Mr Bleaney*, one of his most anthologised pieces, created, in unadorned language and with the use of a few carefully chosen details, the setting of the rented room and the personalities involved:

> This was Mr Bleaney's room. He stayed
> The whole time he was at the Bodies, till
> They moved him. Flowered curtains, thin and frayed ...
>
> Bed, upright chair, sixty-watt bulb, no hook
> Behind the door, no room for books or bags.

As many of Larkin's poems do, *Mr Bleaney* moved from the particular scene to a wider view and so to a more universal significance. It also used a traditional four-line stanza with ease and flexibility.

People and city-scapes are perhaps Larkin's most frequent subjects, but he also wrote about the natural world with real empathy. Animals in particular he often saw as victims of man's selfishness. There was the painful picture of the dying rabbit in *Myxomatosis* and in *At Grass* he showed sympathy for the old horses, who were forced to spend their youth being driven round a race course for man's entertainment. It was only now that they

> stand at ease,
> Or gallop for what must be joy,
> And not a fieldglass sees them home.

Larkin is often thought of as having a pessimistic outlook and death was certainly a subject that constantly engaged him. He admitted that he was afraid of dying, of 'endless extinction', and this threat is found in poems such as *An Arundel Tomb*, *The Building, Hospital Visits* and in his last poem *Aubade*, where he wrote that

the dread
Of dying, and being dead,
Flashes afresh to hold and horrify.

At the end however he expressed a certain stoicism; the fact that life still goes on and 'Work has to be done.'

Throughout his career Larkin wrote with perception and sensitivity, but in a style that made his ideas readily accessible. He disliked the trend to make poetry difficult, influenced perhaps by his upbringing in the industrial midlands, which gave him an appreciation of the direct language of ordinary working people. He was said to have declared that "Deprivation is to me what daffodils are to Wordsworth". Certainly life in the mid-twentieth century for the man on the street has been celebrated by him.

Since his death his popularity has resulted in several television programmes on his life and work, a controversial biography by Andrew Motion, and Tom Courtney's one-man play *Pretending to be Me*. In life his personality often appeared unappealing, but his poetry continues to fascinate.

D H Lawrence (1885 – 1930)

"I never saw a wild thing sorry for itself. A small bird will drop frozen dead from a bough without ever having felt sorry for itself."

David Herbert Richards Lawrence was born in Eastwood in Nottinghamshire, England, the fourth child of a miner and a former schoolmistress, which gave him the working-class background and setting for many of his novels. The tension between his parents surely informed his writings of class tensions.

Although he produced nearly 800 poems, he was better known for his novels, the most famous being *Lady Chatterley's Lover*, which was banned in England due to concerns over its sex scenes and coarse language. The book was largely about a search for integrity and wholeness and it dealt with love and personal relationships. The lovers were a married aristocratic female and a married working class male and therefore considered morally reprehensible adulterers at the time.

In 1959 the censorship laws concerning obscenity were changed slightly in England to allow publishing of explicit scenes if they could be shown to be of literary merit. At once Penguin published *Lady Chatterley's Lover* (written in 1928), which led to the Lady Chatterley Trial in 1960. The court ruled in favour of the publisher. This was a landmark victory for freedom of speech within writing. It also ensured Lawrence's popularity with a wider public and his work began to be included on school and university English literature syllabuses.

However, it should not be forgotten that by then Lawrence was long dead – during his later life he endured harsh criticism and the widespread censorship of his work. In 1928, the book only had a limited private printing in Florence. It was also one of the final products of his career, when he had developed his literary skills to a high degree. In his writings he concerned himself with the dehumanizing effects of modernisation and industrialisation. He was much influenced by Freud's writings on psychoanalysis, and felt that the puritanical culture of England was the basic cause of humanity's unhappiness. Like Freud, Lawrence saw sexual passion as being the core of all human activities.

He wrote thirteen novels, many short stories, non-fiction titles and articles of literary criticism. His writing spanned a broad range, from travel books to metaphysics and symbolism, from poetry to prose and even plays.

His novel *Sons and Lovers* was a fine piece of writing, with its background of the Nottinghamshire coalfields, and it painted a very moving picture of family relationships. His two most celebrated novels, *The Rainbow* and *Women in Love*, dealt with two sisters and their discovery of different facets of the world around them. Lawrence was often a little humourless, with no sense of absurdity, but he had an astute command of English, clear and exact for his purposes. He could create atmosphere and convey an understanding of the inner self with startling clarity.

He said there was a struggle in everyone for a verbal consciousness of the inner life: "Every speck of protoplasm, every living cell is conscious, and all the time they give off a stream of consciousness which flows among the nerves and keeps us spontaneously alive."

Lawrence believed that we needed to restore our emphasis on the body to resist the slow process of over-emphasis on the mind prevalent in western civilization. In this he was a proponent of modernism and was seen as a visionary during the 'love culture' of the 1960s.

He performed well at school, but upon leaving to begin clerical work was struck down with pneumonia. After convalescing he became a pupil teacher and then studied for his teaching certificate. At this time he was working on his novel *The White Peacock* and he won a short story competition.

Once qualified, he took a teaching post in London and continued writing. His poetry was noticed by an influential editor. He was commissioned to write a short story for a magazine, which a London publisher read and so asked Lawrence for more of his work. On the strength of this, he completed his first novel whilst still working as a teacher.

Then his mother died. He was deeply grieved by her passing. He began work on his second novel *Trespassers*, based on a friend's intimate diaries about an unhappy love affair. At the time he had also started writing *Sons and Lovers*. He contracted pneumonia again. After recovering, he decided to abandon teaching to commit himself fully to writing.

Soon after this he met Frieda Weekley, who was six years older than him. She had three children and was married to Lawrence's former professor. They eloped to Germany, where he was arrested as a British spy before being released. They spent their honeymoon in a small hamlet south of Munich, a time that inspired Lawrence's series of love poems entitled *Look! We Have Come Through*. Then they walked across the Alps to Italy. They settled in a cottage on the west coast and he worked on manuscripts of *The Rainbow* and *Women in Love*. When Weekley finally obtained her divorce they returned to England and were married in 1914, at the outbreak of World War One.

Weekley had German parents and Lawrence was openly disapproving of the military so they were viewed with suspicion in wartime England. After constant harassment by the military authorities, Lawrence was forced to leave Cornwall, and he was compelled by poverty to shift his home over and over. Life was hard for him and his wife. Publication of *The Rainbow* was censored. *Women in Love* dramatised the destructive features of civilisation and although it was later recognised as a great English novel, it was too bleak and bitter to be sold during the wartime.

He left England and followed his wanderlust around the world, moving at first to Italy then Austria and drawing on his travels to fuel his new novels. He also wrote poems about the natural world which were published as *Birds, Beasts and Flowers*.

They emigrated to the United States in 1922. There they bought a ranch in New Mexico in exchange for the manuscript of *Sons of Lovers*. They were hoping to establish a utopian community but in 1925 Lawrence suffered a near fatal attack of malaria and tuberculosis and he was advised to return to Europe. He was in very poor health and moved to a villa in Northern Italy where he wrote his last few works including various versions of *Lady Chatterley's Lover* and a defence of the novel against those who sought to suppress it.

He renewed his interest in oil painting. His last work was a reflection on the Book of Revelation, *Apocalypse.*

As well as being an important novelist, he was one of the twentieth century's major poets. He tended to write quite long poems, in a free verse form, and his use of language and assonance is remarkably effective. There is no sentimentality in Lawrence's poetry and his poems are very effective when spoken aloud because of this directness.

Marina Lewycka (1946 – present)
"I knew that this was my last chance: if this one didn't get published, I'd give up."

Marina Lewycka was born in a refugee camp in Kiel in Germany at the end of the Second World War. At a young age her father brought her to England. Because of this she is able to observe Britain both as an insider and an outsider and to capture something relevant and necessary about contemporary Britain and its mix of cultures.

She studied at Keele University and went on to teach in various institutions before a long-term post lecturing Media Studies and Public Relations at Sheffield Hallam University. For decades what she wrote remained unpublished, earning her only rejection letters. In an interview she commented, "The feeling of rejection, when you have put years of your life into something, is so intense, that you have to be both brave and mad to do it again."

She completed an MA in Creative Writing which had the benefit of forcing her to produce a certain amount of writing every week, and to show it to other people. Once she started to receive positive feedback from her tutors and fellow students, it gave her the confidence to persevere with something that she was afraid might be too weird and wacky to get published. The course also put her in touch with a literary agent (one of the moderators). She finally found a publisher with her 'debut' novel, *A Short History of Tractors in Ukranian*, in 2005, at the age of 58.

It became a worldwide hit. The story was influenced by her family life and conversations she had with her mother before she died. Although it began as a memoir Lewycka soon realised that she didn't have enough information about her family to make a book and so it grew into a work of fiction. The dark family comedy included insights that Lewycka gained from researching and writing several short books of practical advice for caring for the elderly.

Of being published, Lewycka said, "It was amazing – it was like a door opening into a magic room – a room outside of which I had stood for years, pressing my nose against the window, wondering how I was going to get in."

A Short History of Tractors in Ukranian won many awards. It was long-listed for the Man Booker Prize and shortlisted for the Orange Prize for Fiction. It told of two sisters trying to rescue their father from the clutches of a Ukranian divorcee. The oddball title caused Amazon to classify the book in the 'agriculture' section at first. The title came from the 'story within a story', a book that the father was writing about the role of tractors in Marxist and capitalist economies.

A Short History of Tractors in Ukranian has been widely translated and is celebrated for its witty blend of comedy and desperation. Ironically it encountered some hostility from Ukranian reviewers and reluctance regarding its translation into Ukranian. This may have something to do with the fact that the Ukraine doesn't wish to be famous for a story about an incontinent old man and a woman with enormous breasts.

Lewycka doesn't consider the story patronising; she believes that it is important for us to be able to laugh at human foibles, and she chooses to write the truth as she sees it rather than what may be politically correct.

She was motivated in part by the fact that although Ukrainians have lived in England in quite large numbers since the Second World War, they are largely invisible; their difficult lives are simply unknown to most people. She admits that Eastern European humour is often very dark as it is the humour of people used to coping with terrible circumstances.

For her second book she drew on her memories of when she was young and had worked with her mother as a pea-picker in Lincolnshire. She used this experience to write a story about the migrant workers from Eastern Europe who worked in the strawberry fields of Kent. This was *Two Caravans* (published in the United States as *Strawberry Fields*). It traced the characters' lives, loves and battle to survive and had a similar stark satirical style to her first book. Again it presented the voice of immigrants. It was a shrewd observation about the waste inflicted by prejudice and injustice.

She believes that every writer she has read has influenced her in some way. Amongst the most memorable, she says that she 'loves James Joyce's lists, Shakespeare's interplay between comedy and tragedy, Salman Rushdie's way with foreign English and John Donne's juxtaposition of love and science'.

Gareth Owen (1936 – present)
"Computer games don't affect kids, I mean if Pac Man affected us as kids, we'd all be running around in darkened rooms, munching pills and listening to repetitive music."

Gareth Owen was born in Ainsdale, England in 1936. Although known especially as a poet and writer, Owen is also a teacher, performer, director and radio presenter. He has worked off Broadway and has had connections in the music business.

By his own admission Owen did not excel academically although he was always good at English. He left school at the age of sixteen. He joined the Merchant Navy for four years. Following this, Owen had various jobs including factory work and gardening. He eventually found his way to London.

There he enrolled at Goldsmiths College, part of the University of London. He made good friends whilst at the college and became involved with the campus theatre. He developed interests in Greek literature as well as in Shakespeare. Following his graduation, Owen took up his first teaching post at a Secondary school in East London and then became Head of English and Drama.

In 1964, he moved to Birmingham where he taught drama at a College of Education. He remained there for the next sixteen years. As well as writing, Owen also performed in radio plays, did voice-over work for television, ran theatre workshops and performed his own work, as well as others' poetry, around the country. In the 1990s Owen worked as a Presenter for the BBC Radio Four programme, Poetry Please. He now lives in the remote marches of Wales. He has long been a keen supporter of Everton, and includes soccer, reading, music, the theatre and cinema amongst his interests.

When he was twelve, Gareth Owen decided he wanted to become a writer, because he imagined it was glamorous. However, it was only when he was teaching at the secondary school that he started to write poetry. He had found that there was little poetry to interest the boys at his school. He decided he should write about everyday things in everyday situations to capture their imaginations. It was during this time that *Salford Road* began to take shape.

In 1970 the first of these poems went into print in a publication called *Wordscapes*. In 1979 *Salford Road* was published in hard-back. In the meantime, Owen was busy writing plays for adults and children. Feeling that he would like 'a change of direction', Owen began reading a chapter each week from a story that he was writing to a group of schoolchildren. Before long, the book entitled *The Final Test* came into being. It was published in 1985 and was runner-up for The Smarties Award.

Then in 1986 followed Owen's second collection of poems, *Song of a City*. This won The Signal Poetry Award and in 1987 *Salford Road* was published in paperback. Owen continued to write books for children in the late 1980s. These included, *The Man with Eyes Like Windows* (1987) and *Never Walk Alone* (1991). In 1989, he also wrote *Douglas The Drummer* and *Ruby and the Dragon* for younger children, followed by *Omelette* in 1990.

In 1995 he released his next collection of poems, *The Fox and the Roundabout*. These poems are aimed at a teenage audience. He was then inspired to write another story, *Rosie No-Name and the Forest of Forgetting* (1997), which was aimed at an older audience. It was allegorical and took us into a world of fantasy. In his radio programmes, *Poetry Please*, as well as appealing to poetry lovers with easily accessible poetry, Owen also sought to bring more exacting work to public notice.

Owen's own poetry has been described as accessible and relevant to children and adults alike. On the surface, his poetry is light-hearted, but at a deeper level, it often deals with real issues that are meaningful to the reader. *Salford City* was mainly biographical, and Owen drew from his own childhood. It is what Owen himself describes as "a confessional voice of a boy about ten." A quotation from the Signal Magazine, when referring to *Song of the City*, reads: "They (the poems) assume our attention and merit it." In *Books for Keeps*, *The Fox and the Roundabout* was applauded for the fact that "Children relate very easily to his poems yet they are not read quickly for a laugh and then forgotten."

In Gareth Owen's opinion, children are not very observant and it is necessary to make things real for them. Owen has very clear views about what he is trying to achieve in his writing. He claims that, "If he (a poet) cannot 'sing' he can never really be a poet." Owen says that for him "It begins with the words; the way they yearn towards the condition of music and yet in the hands of the best are paradoxically concrete and specific."

Owen maintains that sounds and rhymes are also important. For it is the vowel sound that "carries the emotional weight of the poem." Once in a while a verse does come magically into his head, but this is only the start and to continue and create a whole poem is the result of hard work. Most of the time he likes to follow the established rules of prosody and indeed he finds this liberating, although he admits that sometimes the rigour of the poem can be better felt through a more relaxed rhythmic pattern.

In his autobiographical website Owen concludes by emphasising the value of the audience. He believes that in the end the writer writes not just for himself, but to try to connect with someone else who will be able to relate to an idea or memory that he has also felt. In other words, "Writing is more to do with memory and recognition than with mere invention."

Edgar Allan Poe (1809 – 1849)

"I became insane, with long intervals of horrible sanity."

Edgar Allan Poe was born in Boston, Massachusetts (USA) in 1809. He is known for his productive but dismal existence, dogged by poverty and cursed by lack of success. Poe's adulthood was a constant struggle against destitution and despair and rounds of self-destructive drinking. His writing was emotionally dark and often morbid, full of abstract beauty and nocturnal themes, touching on universal, deeply rooted fears; in a word – gothic. He is considered to be part of the American

Romantic Movement.

By the time he was three, he'd lost both parents (who were travelling actors) leaving him with feelings of utter abandonment. Young Poe was fortunate to be taken in by prosperous, doting foster parents. He was brought up by John Allan, a tobacco exporter from Richmond, Virginia (USA). Though he was never formally adopted, Edgar Poe inserted his guardian's name into his own. They provided him with an excellent education in Virginia and England, but the relationship ended badly, with his foster mother's death from consumption and Poe's bitter estrangement from his foster father, who cut him off without a cent in late adolescence after he accumulated gambling debts.

In 1827 he paid for the anonymous publication of *Tamerlane and other Poems*. A year later he enlisted in the Army, hoping to find some 'external discipline' and a source of income. He was discharged and tried officers' training at West Point, but was dismissed in 1831.

When he was 27, Poe married his 13-year-old cousin Virginia, whom he had met when he moved into his aunt's household, when Virginia was 9. His brother Henry was also living in the household but he died from tuberculosis soon after Poe moved in. Poe never felt at home anywhere and they moved repeatedly as he chased literary hack work, editing and writing stories and reviews for various literary journals. One such periodical was the Southern Literary Messenger in which he published some of his best stories.

Tales of the Grotesque and Arabesque appeared in 1839; *The Murders in the Rue Morgue* in 1841; *The Gold Bug* in 1843; *The Raven*, the first poem which won him wide popularity, in 1845. Other verse includes: *To Helen, Israfel, The City in the Sea, The Haunted Palace* and *Dreamland* between 1831 and 1844. *Ulalume* appeared in 1847, *For Annie, Annabel Lee* and *The Bells* in 1849. Famous tales include *The Fall of the House of Usher* (1839), *A Descent into the Maelstrom* (1841), *The Masque of The Red Death* and *The Mystery of Marie Roget* (1842), *The Purloined Letter* (1845), *The Cask of Amontillado* and *The Facts in the Case of M. Waldemar* (1846).

His macabre style was dominated by what some consider a tormented obsession with death. Consider this extract from *The Fall of the House of Usher*:

'I looked upon the scene before me – upon the mere house, and the simple landscape features of the domain – upon the bleak walls – upon the vacant eye-like windows – upon a few rank sedges – and upon a few white trunks of decayed trees – with an utter depression of soul which I can compare to no earthly sensation more properly than to the after-dream of the reveller upon opium – the bitter lapse into everyday life – the hideous dropping off of the veil. There was an iciness, a sinking, a sickening of the heart – an unredeemed dreariness of thought which no goading of the imagination could torture into aught of the sublime. What was it – I paused to think – what was it that so unnerved me in the contemplation of the House of Usher?'

Poe also wrote much literary criticism but his discriminating, philosophical, fearless and often sarcastic reviews did not earn him any friends. For his own writing he was much admired by Baudelaire and Dostoevsky and in Britain by Swinburne, Wilde, Rossetti and Yeats. Indeed, Yeats considered Poe to be 'always and for all lands a great lyric poet'. However, in his own lifetime he achieved poor sales; too small an income to survive on.

His wife died from tuberculosis, and two years later he died, aged only 40. It is believed he died from a combination of alcohol poisoning, heart failure and epilepsy. His literary legacy endures in his stories and in his influence on literature, especially the genres of mystery, horror and science fiction. He made an impact on 19th-century French Romantic poetry as well (Baudelaire spent nearly fourteen years translating Poe into French).

His life was a cautionary tale that highlighted the fact that greatness in literature does not necessarily mean greatness in life. He was the first well-known American writer to try to survive on the income of writing alone.

William Shakespeare (1564 – 1616)

"Life's but a walking shadow, a poor player, that struts and frets his hour upon the stage, and then is heard no more; it is a tale told by an idiot, full of sound and fury, signifying nothing."

William Shakespeare lived at a time when drama had been successfully developed into a formal structure. It was also an age of exploration, and he explored the psyches of a wider range of individuals than any other writer before or since. The tension between the highly-structured form and the sympathy for the inner life of his characters enabled him to push back the boundaries of drama to an unprecedented degree. His sense of dramatic structure improved as he wrote, and he stands as a model of economy and precision, both in his thoughts and his manner of expressing them.

Controversy surrounds what little we know of Shakespeare's life. Born and educated in Stratford-upon-Avon (England), the son of middle-class glove-maker John Shakespeare and well-born Mary Arden, Shakespeare married Anne Hathaway and sired three children – Suzannah, Hamnet and Judith.

He moved to London, worked in one of the theatres there, and by the early 1590s he was established as part of the Lord Chamberlain's Men (later known as the King's Men). He wrote some thirty-seven plays before retiring to New Place in Stratford around 1612.

Shakespeare was an actor and is believed to have played roles in his own plays, among them the Ghost in *Hamlet* and Duke Senior in *As You Like It*. He wrote many of his leading roles for the King's Men's leading actor, the flamboyant Richard Burbage. By 1598 Shakespeare was sufficiently prominent to share in the establishment of the new Globe Theatre.

Shakespeare's works include a cycle of history plays covering English history from Richard II to Richard III; a series of Roman tragedies (*Julius Caesar*, *Titus Andronicus*, *Anthony and Cleopatra* and *Coriolanus*); a clutch of comedies including *Twelfth Night*, *The Merchant of Venice*, *The Taming of the Shrew*, *Much Ado About Nothing* and *As You Like It*; the celebrated tragedies *Hamlet*, *Macbeth*, *Othello* and *King Lear*; as well as plays which are less easy to categorise – bitter comedies such as *Measure for Measure* and *Troilus and Cressida* and fables of forgiveness and redemption such as *The Winter's Tale* and *The Tempest*.

Shakespeare is remarkable in that he never presents us with his own opinions in a character's mouth. He always writes the character from the character's own point of view, and the language and vocabulary of each individual is always coherent and consistent. His other remarkable innovation was his characterisation of women.

He has not always been regarded as a great dramatist. There were times when he was considered very poor, even vulgar and crude, and both Dryden and Pope wrote 'improvements' of his plays. Many of his speeches are well-known and countless lines have passed into everyday language.

As well as writing plays, Shakespeare wrote a magnificent collection of sonnets, mysteriously dedicated to Mr W H (clearly a wealthy and good-looking young man) whose identity is the subject of much scholarly debate. Had he not been a playwright, the *Sonnets* and passages of *The Rape of Lucrece* would have placed Shakespeare in the front rank of Elizabethan poets.

Shakespeare has a remarkable vocabulary. Otto Jesperson in *The Growth and Structure of the English Language* gives him 21 000 words against Milton's 8 000 and the *Old Testament's* 4 800. The modern 'educated' person has perhaps 2 000, of which 700 are said to comprise the normal vocabulary of the average individual.

He had become prosperous by the time he retired and died at the age of 54, bequeathing his wife, Anne, his second best bed – a quirky entry in his will which has given rise to fascinated speculation ever since.

Much of Shakespeare's life is shrouded in mystery so it is important that you conduct your own research in order to draw your own conclusions. There are numerous books published on Shakespeare's life, times and works.

John Steinbeck (1902 – 1968)

"I am impelled, not to squeak like a grateful and apologetic mouse, but to roar like a lion out of pride in my profession."

John Steinbeck was born of immigrant American parentage – his father was an accountant and his mother loved the arts. He had a distinguished career as a novelist, short story writer and war correspondent. His literary career began in 1929 with the publication of his first novel, *Cup of Gold*, which was an unsuccessful attempt at romance. His first three novels were unsuccessful and it wasn't until *Tortilla Flat* (1935) that he achieved popularity with a gently humorous story of Mexican-Americans.

He grew up in Salinas Valley in California (USA), where the culture was diverse due to the migratory and immigrant nature of the community. Summers were spent working on ranches and although he attended university he left without obtaining a degree. As he spent considerable time supporting his writing with manual labour, he could describe the lives of the working class with an authentic voice. He went to New York for a few years where he worked as a reporter and construction worker before deciding to dedicate himself to becoming a novelist. He returned to California and began writing.

His favourite book was a collection of legends of King Arthur by Sir Thomas Malory. Steinbeck was married three times and had two sons by his second wife.

His novels were based on historical events of the first half of the 20th century. He highlighted struggling characters, the working classes and immigrant workers during the great Depression. Some of his works, like *In Dubious Battle* (1936), have been described as unrelentingly grim, but he was good at building rich symbolic structures and in giving his characters archetypal qualities whilst writing with a naturalistic style.

He won the Drama Critics' Prize in 1938 for the dramatisation of his novella *Of Mice and Men*. The play was produced in 1937 and was highly regarded for its realistic picture of itinerant labour. It was the tragic story of a disabled farm-hand and the complex bond he formed with another migrant labourer. A powerful and moving book, it has been criticised for a lack of moral vision.

The Grapes of Wrath, written in 1939, told the story of a family taking flight from the arid conditions of the state of Oklahoma to seek a better life in California, and their subsequent exploitation by a ruthless system of agricultural economics. This is probably his most well-known work and was a high point in his career. It was a tribute to humankind's will to survive and a successful example of social protest in fiction. It won a Pulitzer Prize and National Book Award. The writing highlighted Steinbeck's liberal political views and the book was banned from schools and libraries for a short period of time. It was turned into a movie in 1940 (to be later followed on-screen by *Cannery Row, The Pearl* and *East of Eden)*. He also wrote a few scripts directly for movies.

After the success of *The Grapes of Wrath*, he went to Mexico to collect marine life with a biologist and wrote *Sea of Cortez* which is a book on marine biology (which he had studied at Stanford University). His later work covered politics, religion, history and mythology. He wrote some effective government propaganda during World War Two and served as a war correspondent.

After the war he wrote *Cannery Row* (1945), *The Pearl* (1947) and *The Wayward Bus* (1947), which compared to his earlier books were relaxed sentimental works of social criticism. They were followed by three novels which failed to gain critical acclaim, and minor works of entertainment. In all he wrote twenty-five books, including sixteen novels, six non-fiction books and several collections of short stories.

In 1962 John Steinbeck was awarded the prestigious Nobel Prize for Literature. In his acceptance speech he is quoted as saying: "... the writer is delegated to declare and to celebrate man's proven capacity for greatness of heart and spirit – for gallantry in defeat, for courage, compassion and love. In the endless war against weakness and despair, these are the bright rally flags of hope and of emulation. I hold that a writer who does not passionately believe in the perfectibility of man has no dedication nor any membership in literature."

Rose Tremain (1943 – present)

"The process of rewriting is enjoyable, because you're not in that existential panic when you don't have a novel at all."

Novelist Rose Tremain was born Rosemary Jane Thompson in London in 1943. She is a graduate of the University of East Anglia. Rose Thompson became Rose Tremain when she married her first husband, Jon Tremain in 1971. Their daughter Eleanor was born a year later.

Since her first novel, *Sadler's Birthday*, was published in 1976,

Rose Tremain's literary output has been prolific and diverse. To date she has written eight novels, several collections of short stories, a children's book and a number of television and radio plays.

She was influenced by the writing of William Golding (*Lord of the Flies*) and Gabriel García Márquez (*100 Years of Solitude*) who seek to comprehend situations beyond their own experience through magical realism. Rose Tremain deliberately sets out to explore unknown subjects, trusting her imagination to achieve a thorough understanding for both herself and her reader. Even when the subject matter is serious her writing is both poetic and highly entertaining. Rose Tremain believes keeping to one form stifles creativity and makes a writer stale and repetitive. She readily experiments with unconventional styles and different genres in order to ensure her work is fresh and unpredictable.

Her novels are also multi-themed. In her early novels *Sadler's Birthday* (1976), *Letter to Sister Benedicta* (1978) and *The Cupboard* (1981), ageing and death are the dominant themes interwoven with love in all its forms.

In 1983 Rose Tremain was selected as one of Granta magazine's 'Best of Young British Novelists'. This was to be the first of many such nominations, prizes and awards. In 1984 she was the recipient of the Dylan Thomas Award for short stories – three of which appear in *The Colonel's Daughter and Other Stories* (1984). She also received the Giles Cooper Award for her radio play *Temporary Shelter*.

Dispossession, bereavement and all forms of prejudice are among the many other themes addressed in her writing, as is sensuality, in many guises. Food is seriously appreciated and an over-indulgence in both alcohol and sex bring an entertaining and often humorous realism to Rose Tremain's stories.

The Swimming Pool Season (1985) contains an evocative description of a birthday feast and explores tangled relationships in a sleepy French village. For this novel she received the Angel Literary Award (1985). In 1989 Rose Tremain was the recipient of this award again for *Restoration*, her best-selling historical novel set during the reign of King Charles II, which tells the story of Robert Merivel, a medical student and Court favourite, who falls in love with the King's mistress. Allowing her main character to address the reader directly gave this novel an interesting dimension and appeal. This earned Tremain the Sunday Express Book of the Year Award (1989) as well as a Booker Prize for Fiction short-listing in 1990. *Restoration* was made into a film in 1996 featuring Hugh Grant and Meg Ryan.

Her novel *Sacred Country* (1992), in which a young girl confronts issues of identity and gender, won the James Tait Black Memorial Prize (for fiction) and the Prix Femina Etranger (France). *The Way I Found Her* (1997) was a psychological thriller set in Paris. *Music and Silence* (1999) was a many-themed historical novel set in 17th century Denmark that explores society from multiple viewpoints at the court of King Christian IV. It won the Whitbread Novel Award.

The Colour (2003) is set in 19th century New Zealand during the West Coast gold rush. It tells the story of newlyweds, Joseph and Harriet Blackstone, immigrants in search of a new life, battling against the harshness of a bleak world as well as human frailty. In her latest novel, *The Road Home* (2007) Rose Tremain explores the issue of migration in the present day as she tells the story of an impoverished immigrant struggling to survive while supporting his daughter back home in Eastern Europe.

As lecturer in creative writing at the University of East Anglia (1988 – 1995) Rose Tremain has influenced the styles of many talented young novelists. In 2000 the university awarded her an honorary Doctor of Literature degree and in 2007 she was awarded a CBE (a British order of merit). She has been on the panel of judges for the Booker Prize for Fiction and is a regular reviewer in both the press and on radio.